History or Sleep

Also by Robert Sheppard

Poetry
Returns
Daylight Robbery
The Flashlight Sonata
Transit Depots/Empty Diaries
    (with John Seed [text] and Patricia Farrell [images])
Empty Diaries
The Lores
The Anti-Orpheus: a notebook *
Tin Pan Arcadia
Hymns to the God in which My Typewriter Believes
Complete Twentieth Century Blues
Warrant Error *
Berlin Bursts *
The Given
A Translated Man *
Words Out of Time
Unfinish

Fiction
The Only Life

Edited
Floating Capital: New Poets from London (with Adrian Clarke)
News for the Ear: A Homage to Roy Fisher (with Peter Robinson)
The Salt Companion to Lee Harwood
The Door at Taldir: Selected Poems of Paul Evans *

Criticism
Far Language: Poetics and Linguistically Innovative Poetry 1978-1997
The Poetry of Saying: British Poetry and Its Discontents 1950-2000
Iain Sinclair
When Bad Times Made for Good Poetry *
The Meaning of Form in Contemporary Innovative Poetry (forthcoming)

* Titles from Shearsman Books

Robert Sheppard

History or Sleep

—*Selected Poems*—

Shearsman Books

First published in the United Kingdom in 2015 by
Shearsman Books
50 Westons Hill Drive
Emersons Green
BRISTOL
BS16 7DF

Shearsman Books Ltd Registered Office
30–31 St. James Place, Mangotsfield, Bristol BS16 9JB
(this address not for correspondence)

www.shearsman.com

ISBN 978-1-84861-398-0

Copyright © Robert Sheppard, 2015.
The right of Robert Sheppard to be identified as the author
of this work has been asserted by him in accordance with the
Copyrights, Designs and Patents Act of 1988.
All rights reserved.

ACKNOWLEDGEMENTS

The poems in this selection were most recently collected in the following publications, where previous magazine, pamphlet and book publications are gratefully acknowledged: *Returns, Looking North, Daylight Robbery, Codes and Diodes, The Anti-Orpheus: A Notebook, Hymns to the God in which My Typewriter Believes, Complete Twentieth Century Blues, Warrant Error, The Given, Berlin Bursts, A Translated Man, Words Out of Time, The Drop*, and on *Pages (robertsheppard. blogspot.com)*.

All texts written 1990-2000 formed part of a time-based network of texts, 'Twentieth Century Blues', published as *Complete Twentieth Century Blues* (2008), including poetics and detailed index of its 75 parts and its 97 'strands'; additionally, some earlier texts were introduced into the numbering. For this selection, I have omitted this schema. The appearance of a number of poems in both *Tin Pan Arcadia* and *Complete Twentieth Century Blues* has allowed me to be severe with their de-selection and re-packaging here.

Contents

Round Midnight	9
One for William Carlos Williams	10
Returns	11
Strategies	15
Twin Poem	17
from The Hungry Years: an Unwriting	19
from Mesopotamia	22
The Materialisation of Soap 1947	25
Looking North 2	26
Internal Exile	28
Living Daylights	33
Coming Down from St George's Hill	38
His Furious Skip	41
Three Poems by Wayne Pratt:	
from The Penguin Book of British Parrots	46
The Magnetic Letter	49
Melting Borders	50
from Smokestack Lightning	51
from Killing Boxes	53
Fucking Time	56
from Empty Diaries 1901-1990	59
from The Lores	69
History or Sleep	79
Three Hundred Word Sonnets	
from The Lores, Book 8	90
from Entries: Empty Diary 1996	91
Small Voice 1	92
The Push Up Combat Bikini: Empty Diary 2000	93
A Voice Without	94
Only the Eyes are Left	95
Parody and Pastoral	96
from Reading *The Reader*	97
National Security, Huyton 1940	101
Three Figures Climb	103

Erotic Elegy	104
Prison Camp Violin, Riga	106
from Berlin Bursts	108
from Warrant Error	112
Four Poems Against Death	124
Another Poem	129
Yet Another Poem	130
As Yet Untitled Poem	131
The Given, part one	132
from Arrival	137
Standing by	138
Fictional Poems from *A Translated Man*:	
from The Masks	139
from The Light	143
from EUOIA	144

*To the memory of Lee Harwood
and for Scott Thurston*

Round Midnight

Stan Tracey: tribute to Thelonious Monk

The varnished Bechstein
has been polished beyond perfection:
two rows of mirrored ivories
grinning
under a spotlight.

                              He stabs
his first jagged chord, pricking it
with stray notes. But the ghost's hands
are also at their keyboard, a left
knuckling his right, exactly.

The jumping hands below his bowed head
flesh an illusion, filling
the punched hollows as he watches.

Both pairs
have followed this dance too often
to break formation with the other.

But if one played a sharp where the other
played a flat
we might witness chaos – or invention.

One for William Carlos Williams

A slender stem of water,
surfacing, twists
into a thin-throated flower,
and wavers in the vibrant gulf –

where words set
free are tuned-up, resonant,
to the cry of the world at the poem's edge:
to the truant breeze
on our faces, carrying
the scent of sage as rain shakes it
free from the trembling leaves;

while the mind, stirred
by the wild names
of the common flowers, wakes
and flares.

Returns

1

Rain beats upon me the measure
of the real. Slothfully
an idiot paperboy is moving along the wet street.
Time and again he's erased from the drafts
of my poems, but is now allowed
to stay: humping up the garden paths,
dumbly glimpsing at rolled headlines
between houses. It is spring.

You step into the poem, slide
between its cool sheets. When I'm with you
I think about the poem. When I'm
writing I'm thinking of you
as palpable as memory, somewhere
the other side of sense. The touch
of your hand
becomes almost a memory as you enter
a blank scenario. The idiot paperboy
with the orange bag of evening
papers, leaves the poem.

What is this rainbow, or that
twin rainbow we saw
one confused afternoon, but a wonder
of discriminations cutting
upon a knife-edge of sunlight, trained
in the self-evidence of a beautiful day. Spring
moves towards summer
as night pulls away the rind of dusk.
Public persons return to become private
people again.

You come into the room and the poem follows
to where private words
are found sheltering in cramped parentheses
like spoons in bed, making little sense.
Pausing before the curtains you watch sudden rain
striking out the day, a speckled impression
on the window.

2

Four unmodernised sash windows,
sixteen panes of glass in each, shatter
your reflection with neat
disregard, as you pass.

A face veiled by a curtain or ghosting
the vacancy of the dark room
fills one entire pane; the squared world
plays its forms on this face which cannot see it.

You step out of this grid, return
to the public spectrum of plain eyes,
and are gone about your business –
which is not the business of the poem.

3

People walk in the park as usual,
unrestrained by the nicknames that follow
on a withering glance.
                              You walk to the place
where you are turned inside-out
like an empty pocket at each fresh
proposition. The only sign of life
is a scaled-down voice through a grille,

its hot breath on a protective screen:
a pellicle of fear. Somebody
is practising on a drum,
a rolling intermittent, persistence; somewhere
just out of range, lies perfect chaos.

Small children in summer clothes
are running towards a frozen stream
on somebody else's afternoon; no wind
stirs in this fresco world, carved into granite silence.

This should be a poem of loss
and longing. It is not a question
of working it out, but of drawing it in
through the senses, and of letting something happen
and go on happening, shifting
on the slurry of tongues.

4

Your eyelids flicker at the edge of waking
as I speak into your dream, turning it
in ways neither of us
may choose. But the movement
of the eyes is itself
the measure, an index of your waking hours
which still has to find,
at the root of what's always been there,
what's never been there; the chance excess
of a flash of renewed memory,
the scent of something
evaporating on the hob of the mind:
the touch of phosphorescence, scooping
luminous handfuls of its quicksilver-body
from the warm water, green sparks at your fingertips.
The sound of oars batting ghost-waves across

the still surface of the river
fills an empty ear. When you are gone the room
is locked into dumb significance. Nothing
moves unless I stretch across
its creased planes of habit. The room,
when I am gone, is folded
into memory. There are many rooms,
many poems. But there is only one you,
fracturing the world like a prism. Two bees
hum from flower to flower on the
aubrietia, nosing into each
as they hang upside-down,
silently gathering for a second. There
is no sense in pointing at the flowers. The dream
returns throughout the day, a prickling ripple
along the spine of this surface that buoys you up –
then breaks beneath you. Particles of spray
sting the eyes.

Strategies

Vagrant sun, with heavy bags of cloud to sleep on. Out cold on the park bench in the afternoon, newsprint comes off on your skin; sweat is ink. You are a stencil, ready to print upon whatever it is that will rub against you. Your grubby opinions.

Jesus, sweating on his cross in the schoolyard. Or up there, where the garden narrows to a dung-heap. Anywhere you choose. Children playing in the street after the massacre, chalking lines around one another's make-believe corpses.

Einstein's pickled brain: study this crinkled walnut to determine the contours of genius. The sounds of the molecules shuffling restlessly through the fabric of the Turin Shroud. A cluster of electric bulbs in a fake chandelier, wired in parallel, winks slyly at the stiff dancers below. A photograph of Einstein poking his tongue out.

The kernel of the skull filled with wine vinegar. Duck! Here comes another squashy opinion, lucid while it flies, messy on impact. A vegetable stuffed with broken beer glasses and sawdust. Then another. And another.

Pick up the man with his arm in a sling, struggling like a woodlouse to get upright, on the pavement over from Yates' Wine Lodge. Someone's given him a proper squashed tomato. Pick him up, clean up your metaphors, and be off with you.

Prostitutes: always by a canal or a brewery, somewhere with 'atmosphere'. Steps built for sitting on; walls for leaning against. The rest is flooded with a darkness that brims at the edges of the lit streets.

Watch the chisel chipping away the caul, as you sit for the monument that will tower, larger than life, over your tomb. Natural wastage: you feel suddenly redundant, feel the pressure of all the others wishing themselves into your shoes. The drunk is a fallen statue, toppled from eminence, concussed on the bench. He wakes into a landscape of empty bottles, over which he has been granted dominion. He'll stagger downhill to the stone troughs, the horse-coffins.

Small miracles: poke the nozzle of the instrument into the ears and look through the eye-piece. What do the patterns you see mean? The de-caffeinated coffee bean. The can of non-alcoholic cider. Mix the contents of the bottle with the warm specimen and watch it change colour. Small wonder.

He is an excrescence of the architecture, where the alleys are too narrow. He was snagged off by some violent blow, some wild thrashing against authority. After the public whipping there can be no shame. Why did the singer melt into a brown liquid before the surprised audience? Escapologist.

Still-born action: the imploding woman in the diving bell. The virgin birth in the iron lung. With a ripple of despair, the wheezing legend in the oxygen tent turns to stone.

Twin Poem

A gloss between the lines
Identical to ours. This is the city
Of the stories you tell in narrowing
Testimony. Fragmentary pauses and shifts
Carried into the mind make credible things:
The light shimmering in the heat.
It is the pulsing gift which
Wakes in you a forgotten desire.
You will walk through the poem as though
Unfamiliar in that familiar life.

The executions become routine
But they are four hundred years too late
And in the wrong poem.
You watch me swallowed
Like an alien word that will not
Rise to love you wordlessly. Memory
Of this instant goes
Counterbeat to drum me out
To the regime of this place. People
Stride through the dark streets,
The squinted prose
The fifty men were hanged on
By the judicious wind.
Dreams stir and I
Lose their meanings in work so secret
A voice rises to lyrical soliloquy.

Make a world for you –
Only the promise of that world
Will be effaced
Before its recoil, silenced by the mind
Into its milky glare. The provisional
Government of each new word

Sets the bond men free.
I have given you eyes
Down there in creation. You're stopped
In the poem the sentence before
A roaring plea for possession and release,
An open verdict. When the words die, we die.

from The Hungry Years: an Unwriting

for Lee Harwood

1

He had no need of a name
Or further identity. You will be asked
To point a finger at that
Giver of bounties,
Make a gesture as if drinking from an
Invisible glass of beer and then
Give a swift signal of dismissal, as if to say
What's it worth then, boys?
Herself she had called by to
Imagine the scene:
You are called, late,
At twelve-thirty. You see him
Sitting implacable,
Well groomed, but without
Chatting a little,
A brittle frosty impatience
Between you. The signing hall
Is empty, barely
Visible with the strip lighting.
From the waiting benches
Back to the desk, she sits
Refusing to write.
She stares at the document
Incapably slurred this afternoon.
He enters, singing in a deep
Wavering voice. He topples,
Makes jokes about the politicians,
As if he's forgotten what
He was there for.

4

Drunken youths from the Top Rank
Pressing arrested if broad
And the speedy punks from the Resource Centre.
A year passed. He was sitting alone
In the Belvedere, a beach pub,
Taking occasional sips
From his cold beer. It was late –
Pissed against a sea wall
Giving itself over to the still suntanned tramps.
Each holds an image of ideal female perfection
O is an obvious example.
Tarpaulin rattles
Sash window wind sweeps up
Rocking the moment fire the
Certain man. It's your story
I bet! says the man I am interviewing.
People rush in; the supervisor calms her.
Noisy foreign students in their
Belt loops, not knowing quite what to do
As the embarrassed policemen
Lead her away: at work at bay
Black psychiatrist she walked white
Like a coma. Only half the story
A couple of tortuous signs. If
You interviewed a certain man
On June 21 1978, you will
Foolishly answer yes.

6

He will take a bounding
Leap as he crosses my mind, but
Far from being a loose screw, he is a vital cog
Out above the signing boxes.
The sight of a squashed tomato on her plate
Peppered references to
Further identity. Her open secret
Is no single story; I am playing
The part of all of those girls
Lining up outside the Dyke Road hospital,
Ripe for weeding,
And about three hundred new ones
The other side of your desk.
Fucking useless whore!
He screams at the girl,
Huge trembling body.
He came inside me four
Restless nights under the pier,
Taking our time in a world
Of crowded streets in tiny rooms.
Huddled plots had later shook her bed
Alone with the darkened story slowly pausing.
To point a finger at that
Trumpeter practising
With horrible people in here,
They had to break the door down –
And she tried to kill herself
Nervous at its
Keep with her pale sash window.

from Mesopotamia

1. I am thinking of someone. By the looks of the photo

I dread to look behind me in case I've lost that parallax trickery, running the flickering rows. Adventures are few: a storm during which a chap became so sea-sick they had to remove his future memoirs down the rubber tube, though I couldn't then recognise them as such. Blank cards flicker before my eyes: the ritual Arab girl, shot by a sniper, now bones and tattered uniform. I am still able to recall the earlier girl, her eyes closed. She is the reason why, when you arrive at her, I have gone to locate the disembodied night. I can see clearly his writing skull demanding explanations. Some words it is acceptable to kill, others it is not: an empty diary for the year 1900. The unfortunate Meredith, waking at dawn on the sweat-drenched mattress, offended Arab bordello etiquette. Buffalo Bill settles down, in his suffering, to defend it. 'Memory,' he quips to posterity, 'will clear that sky of cloud!'

2. Y.M.C.A. Billiards

The women had their orders; while the chieftain slept, they were to remove the eyes of the ragged whores, ready for something that limits chaos to ruin my story to pause increasingly often. Render your fugitive memory of having been there, before any part of it fades from your world. The Death Arab speaks to him in a dream in which she becomes snake-nippled Cleopatra: the crumpling and smoothing of oriental silks! They remove this mess from your world so you won't have a map of the British Empire in the 1909 Atlas. Sometimes when I am singing for the people under siege in a Turkish trench, billowing discarnate smoke floats through imperfect shade, but let's hope our camouflage is more convincing than the tent. When I look up from the paragraph he dictates, rising behind the scenes on the edge of Mesopotamia, limpid-eyed enemies knock at the door, invisible fingers, rather than Meredith's, fleshing a chord.

3. To Georgina with Love from Hugh Some K'nut Ah What

Walking round the compound, the dirty beggars let the dogs fight each other to death. He dictates blank cards, the mess pianola slowing, unfleshed dances before the sinking night sounds – laughter, crying, music – that drift on horses' hooves and camels at their eyes. Within, this peep show delinquency: the dim mass of the adversaries dressing; no, that is somebody else's stomach wound which she holds to his lips, filling the shafts of sunlight that had not been there. My grandfather took me to the circus to see Buffalo Bill: at the centre stood a bamboo stake that had not been used in the campaign against the savages. I take the table knife from beside my plate. A tray falls from the painted backcloth behind me; knives, voluminous trousers and savage instinct ordering the mind in its looking. The man who made the piano roll is dead.

4. Graveyard – Mesopotamia Mahinah, Where British troops are buried only

A third soldier chanced a futile dash to the well; after the battle he would enter blank course remains because of the flies. The woman stood staring at me as though I were a problem to be solved, but then I sensed myself slowing until I had actually my storylines of gravestones at Mahinah reduced to clay. For people under siege in writing my story, he becomes somebody else, eyes closed, trying the leopard skin which the settled natives do not possess. Screech owl. Bill always keeps his boots on to fuck, wears his gun in the bath; a bullet had taken his thumbnail away and it never re-grew. You know you've done something in the few minutes since her back concealed a thick mobile in his tent, because he moves like a beggar, hoisted by two giant warriors, each gripping an arm, while he touches her buttocks, dimpled with fat, on the mattress, her back arched in anticipation of a man looking through a keyhole. There's a little switch here that completes the screaming of a young deserter, but his vacant eyes, his clenched fists, his splayed feet, give nothing away.

5. This is a squad of fellows on C.B. for going to Church Some few Sundays ago. All A.S.C.

The other Buffalo Bill settles down in his tent; he already moves as though he is remembered in a volume by his brother, Thomas, so I may never have to defend it. After several impromptu attempts at burial, they are standing up the spirit; we left it there, capable, under the crust of the road. Hollows in those emaciated, pitiful faces, as if printed softly on a fan. The man stunned on the edge of the Turkish trench, as he is about to drop down with his knife. A fresh constellation drifted on the heat, effervescently. Granule-clouds refracted sunlight at dawn and dusk, a ruby luminescence across the sky, reflecting on your face.... No, that was somebody else's future, a scintilla behind bandages and linen until that, too, fades into letters that I cannot combine. Blink above the snaking looking pianola I can rubber restless floats back to the blinding sand, returning to find a man looking through an empty courtyard and the distant blue of the mountains, as if softly printed on a portable screen.

7. Budhists Temple

A figure was leaning against the wall, owl eyes of the death-sport flickering at her fists, affording a view of the jumping scene. Did you suspect, stiffening in your pose, how might that blur of moving flesh have appeared on your face? Buffalo Bill stabbed by seductress, death on London pavements. I turn the handle and the cards begin to flick, recapturing the Garden of Eden, the flies, the mosquitoes and the heat. You step behind my eyes and enter the tunnel of her gaze. One step backwards, and you're gone, waking to a dream of dawn, over which wild cat's eyes, carved into the arm of the chair, close her head. She turns away to reveal a veined neck, set between the cool brass. No, that was somebody trying to locate the morning – my chest covered with flies – a history of sensation on the streets. You're here because that same courtyard, or so I fancied, was the studied flight of stairs until I can take only one sentence at a time. The peep show stilled at the word halting.

The Materialisation of Soap 1947

Suspicion in the capital: the ecstasy
Of austerity rationing the uniforms.
It must be like air, natural and free,
But there's a shortage of nature in this
Land of torrents and the surrounding seas.
What is happening? He used to *prefer* words!
Feed me a well-trimmed cut of news.
We couldn't find any wheels, but we're happy,
A well-dressed pair: even on the wireless
You've got to keep up appearances,
Now we yearn for the parks and the azure skies
Of the tottering economies.... Pearl
Opened her palm over the sink to reveal
A fresh bar of soap. She smelt it; her favourite
Scent. She turned the hissing tap, and
The slippery unthought-of object lathered
Her chapped Cinderella hands. All she needed
Was her hero silk-parachuting into
Her perversely dissatisfied embrace. I
Prefer to talk to the dead, well-fed
On scraps that cannot be sold.
They died from Manchuria to Manchester.
I did not want to report this but I did.
The news is that another man has been held.
That much is reliable. Beyond that,
The monochrome world flickers
At the emotive edge of our fake memories:
Two frying morsels on the gas stove.

Looking North 2

Brownswood Park, N4

for Patricia

Skip down the grove – repeat:
A squinted trace of houses.
You cross cautiously, alert to possibilities,
Dirty eyes at you. The woman has
Walked out: desire follows on a breeze
Of diesel. Cement rifts zigzag
The striding woman and her shadow into
The invisible core, break
Destruction through, but explain nothing. Turn it
Over and continue: tumbled heaps of broken paving slabs,
Shadowed balconies, the voices
Of local people, stasis and frame, in
A fragrant haunting that is unlocatable. Music
Plays the theme but the same words assault the place.

Lights leaning the verticals, plunging
Steel and hedgerow nature through
The re-fashioning city: no clues. A figure
Of a man running after a dog in primeval
Survivalist fury! This is the
Beginning of a new civilisation, a
Lightning bolt shooting the wrong way.
A car explodes, film-jammed, runs
Back into the parking bay, where the driver
Gets out, backs off, spattered blue
And brown on a day of dirty water-marks.
A frail imagining in a field of light.

                         : the frame of
A bus-stop in yellow on the tarmac
And a woman, leaning, murder rush
And the taxi call. Everybody has bags, food,
Tranquillity parked, empty, outside the frame.
The day waits, the toes of the people
On its footbrake. Writing leaves the passion-
Jagged houses bending. The sun glosses
This surface to sky-grey, turning ice-floe rubbish
For the twisting road. There are many junctions.
Steam and glass produce a world
To drop your own worst dreams
On your head, framed as paradigm.
This is value stamped onto light:
Distance thinning the woman. Perspective
Shoots once and the whole city lays siege.

The house which functions as your second
Skull takes on a symbolism it cannot hold:
Black iron steps and railings
Between platforms. Patch off
Into disorder, hands in forgotten hands, as she
Passes through a waking eyeline, flickered
To scratch-lines. The day silvers
The ironwork, up to the boiling-point of incident –
Think so fast that something happens, tipping
The ladder into allegory: a mind
Privately focussed upon
The jutting angle and the limpid pool.
Roots at the bricking-line: this is no place
For an eye like yours. This is the working out
Of Hackney, speckles of brick and black which
Do not configure…

Internal Exile

> *Writing is impossible without some kind of exile*
> Julia Kristeva

1

Out from germ-warm subterranean wind into
Business having just been, or about to be.
Hyphens, dashes, asterisks, strokes:
The silver number has been screwed. Red
Flag: blue light. One moment the man stands
With his arms tied behind his back; the next he falls
Head first from our chronicle. Pictures have pictures.
You are the real hero. The image –
That was like walking into somebody else's poem.
A public zipper porched shadow action. Heroes
Standing under cardboard captions. Masculinity sells
History: four guards on this side, four
On the other, changing according to
House demands. All the victims' outfits were
Manufactured by the Enemy. It was a fantastic
Feeling, going up stage and turning around for all
The judges. Her writing is content. Watches sold
Doubt as her underhand life expressed the
Heresies. Her clothes burn, turning stories,
Can add fur sovereign meaning
To line-sewn memory dust. Don't open the door; shut
Your eyes. To slam these columns you took this out.
The shimmering architectural fantasy
Of a slum, purpose built. Entry to that soft-furnished
Dream, riots hanging like petrol vapour
Over the black plastic rubbish bags,
Electric train-flashes crossing the page, from one of the
Languages which blows across Europe like ill-wind.
Bombs implode as a warning underscoring
The essential sentence. He says my

Mind is always somewhere else when I
Kiss her. This sentence is a variation. She's
Out on the porch, testing the day, transforming
Not only her, but the text, from which she
Could never be exiled. As soon as I write 'the world',
It doesn't invert. Poverty less plentiful
But obscured by wealth and well-being.
The systems began to fail, in domestic adjustment.
The Chinese trains were nicer than the Russian ones.
This sentence is a variation of the next. The flow
Freed from compulsion. Trying to gauge it
All; the woman is not at her mirror. (Skip
A few pages; I will too.) Black girl in a tight leather
Skirt jumps into a waiting passenger-seat:
Pink folds of flesh for his mental
Speculum. I froze and sweated, wanted to burn
The insignia – but who would deck
Themselves in the cloth pages
Of a tattered history? Pretend that some of
The sentences have been removed
Though your meaning heaps. Women desire a war;
Virus men build appearance. Wouldn't you prefer it
As a straight-out? The bike boys zooming in on each
Other's rolling captions? What was once
Familiar is now merely strange. Moving clouds behind
The birds rewind their film of homecoming. Swoop
Loop wires in light. A magpie flicker in dirty
Scruff eye. This has to be learned,
Holding language in suspicion. Posturing
About disaster, style demeans. A cold sore
On a child's mouth predicates a market
Full of bargains. What could she begin to say? How
Will she survive the questioning? Perhaps
It is only the uncurtained window-pane that
Throws the room back at us? Reader:
Worker. Walkman overspill rhythmed by the engine-
Driver's wiper-lashes. Another realism. She

Remarked the dome of her clichéd perception –
An image for later snuff-movie simulations: murder
Leads door to door. The crystal eye set in the wall.
They did not even notice that the effigies were of them.
Replace the object. She makes the unknown turn –
Feels at one moment a gobbet of raw meat in a
Porno film. She goes to the window to cry.

2

Counterpoint. Things hunched in plaster mutually assured desire going blank into the wide-eyed day. Rainshine: blank wives at ashen points. A fur coat pulled out of the water; vanished power in the herringbone stripes. The complication that I was, a tension in myself. Surface woman through a glass letterbox. Dummy texts arranged your life like bales of hay: the evening was to be marched from the script. Story-assassin, in his study. The world is going up, speckled. We buy junk and sell antiques. Norbert hit Renate in the face with a saucepan. Line up for war: she's a beautiful angry female. Norbert dreamt the last sentence. We printed in red any word which could be harnessed to our rule. The five widowed instruments played at the wedding. Girls in soldiers' memories flicker the past. With a female character I can have the other. He is real in a world of dummies. I was made to sit on spikes. He is a kerb-corpse. The writing keeps straining for his scarecrow values. I try to imagine myself living. We govern in the message. A black cylinder meets the spear. Inverted passages and vertiginous corners. Cloud aligned eye: prisoners of war were treated to digging holes. She always claimed her father went to the camps, seeks her sublimation in his end. I was made to sit on spikes. A minor chord failed to split the atom: life between the burning metaphors. Above surface, accidental flesh. Bullet holes in the column. A man in his underpants disappeared from view, as the man with the knife at the throat of another protested against the rules of the game we'd set him. The shadow men prepared for action. More than a form, I retreated to the margins to create myself. I had to destroy it; I began to work, drumming his nerves. Images produced value, misting the houses beyond. Signal shadows people. The girls talked mints; nearby, the mint-man listened, electrified. Ideas surface, cardboard grip. You see if you're not looking, your autism behind make-up. Counterpoint eyes flutter, acting out your own unfinish. He noted, in the gap between two buildings, the type of woman to profitably misunderstand. These are suburban tales: the ghostly glow. Strip ashen zipper: hell victims. The world, like the newspaper photos she treasured, was just killing time. She gave her black lover a photograph of a Somali with severed hands. One language: many voices. The mark of professionalism is conflicting advice. The odd bones of your life matter. The caddy removes a red flag. The plot thins. The question marks. The letterbox is sellotaped. The naughty girl will put herself to bed. She began flirting with her own image. Do you buy the performer with the performance? Ghost markets. You can't step through into the other side, invading the focal arena. Space within? He stops and wills the rest away. The enemies make him zero, jargoned to death. Crude semaphore. Strategic disintegration. Their mermaid ideology – and then scribbled in blue: *GIRLS*. Let's look up at the sky. This is getting normal. She is waiting patiently in a queue. The tanks arrive for one man in a beret. Why was Utopia meat with gristle? Do you want the world – it narrowly missed my briefcase? They are living in temporal consciousness of space. Did you kill your days? Their blind music: a woman with leather stretched across her face. Collapse the bladder of hope. A rough edge divides the vibrant light. Her conversations were electric chairs, fences, wires. Counterpoint contradicted. If you can see your assassin, he becomes your executioner. Historical aphasia: watch the ant-like rioters below. How to avoid being disappointed with our new product? Don't buy it. Burn the books and read the ashes, to make a reader stop her fantasising. If she is naked she is touching. One cracked stair. Why can't one perception *stay* with another? All the blacks have to stand naked against the wall while the police think. I have been writing a journal of sorts. You're lost into a position you cannot fit, while a queue years up shining game. Even to me, there's a future. She includes the sentence, 'She watches her younger self laughing.' My vision of the future has no words. The eye swallows its rhyme. You're certain there's somebody there, tasting her bitterness, biting her tongue. A tortuous voice-over for the final scene. The reader lets go?

3

She's living in the rough
Basement of a condemned house. Street
Level defines a world, its variations
In autonomy. She's a genuine
Answer, designed to put you off. She's
In another time; he is in another gender,
The man with the briefcase, practising
Dance-steps on the platform.
Dry water-colours dust off the stiff washing,
Disrupting any finer feelings he may have had.
You cannot see through the whole. What
Began as art was repeated years later
As a political act. She always wore
Black lipstick, tears in her eyes. Men danced
In fire, did press-ups with guns. Others
Flew to posterity. She burnt her other self,
Teasing out the voyeur's disappointment, the
Beauties of her unbridled
Allegories. The writing returns
To block desire. It's
A world of spies and disclosures; she
Feels his presence in the room with her, scraped
Again across the grain of history. Territory
(Or no territory) on the shit-
Stained canvas of her language:
Her heavy green front door, and its
Dried spattering of blood. Fulfil desire;
KILL IT. It was her statement, her
Trigger on silence. Now
The writing's nearly over the work
Withdraws. Is this a model
Of the world that does not exist, straining
For a new referent? Her prejudices
Owe the world no apology.

Living Daylights

Whitewashed thought flashing articulations those
transparencies
in the daylight skating
on
nobody's dream dodges
into synaesthesia on a
frozen world I
speak
rest my thoughts
too brilliant to bear
contemporary blocks. 'Buy me, my batch
of
old memories, my all nighters

Line streets with shadows which
enter
bedrooms nod into family
scenes
where you can't
afford to gather plausible voice
spilling book swimming
dabs
of man puffs –
caption promo flashes sharp
point recognitions (the face is nobody's
salvage
it) copy translated pulse vision

Creaking shadows others stopped crystalline
loop
phenomena keeping sane eyes
false
steps and they're
at you melody follows

into your thoughts
allegorical
women from costumes
vanish in this presentation
of your life nothing remains except
your
name looking fresh in remodes

Free eyes slide past slipstreaming
drones
responsibility a secret fresco
frozen
bead of sweat
as you discover you're
loathing all dry-
nibbed
blocks of lost
time it's been filmed
and novelised a thousand different ways
say
The other's hinge is loose

Shadows with people sometimes I
wish
I was back in
the
world where movies
were bodies full of
words: Small invasions
ungainly
steps in the
night high crusts of
victory scabs against a star-pricked
bolt:
In the furnace: Phonemes filtered

Tricks trope me) I the
less
refused to answer somebody
else's
voiced phantasy promotion
strap my stripped prickles
were swallowed into
phone-
ins a violated
hiss cut off at
the point of bolts threading the
same
words round each critical block

A cheap chorus of refugee
objects
chanting already dead my
hair
falling forward for
the false steps and
they're at you
No
price tag just
a premonition the straight
proof will be read on my
body
by the lover, doctor, mortician

You cannot elope with yourself
cannot
retreat world (retreat face)
broadcast
secrets but dissemble
in a stolen book
between the capital
letters
and the sparkle

drench explosion still sheens
tomorrow (a spray of bargain basement
postmodernism
brackets off the strange bar

Vowels in tears under mugger
sprays
initial missile shimmering symbol
wire
its lurid splash
on paper lips the
pen. Phonemed ghettoes,
speculative
blanks, 'Meet me
by the floral clock
and I will try to explain –
watch
my eyes become your disgrace

Plausible voice that enemies took
too
literally stepped back explosions
wrenched
him from the
carpet context-hatred spills
onto world shimmering
with
things to soap
your authority smoothed over
the cracks by denying his fresh
bit
of fluff on the scene

Long shadows allegorical on the
sand
expressive gestures stolen from
news

oil it lifts
and real tears stream
down artifice spilling
beans
women glitter, men
glow, shadows catching daylight
falling from windows crowding the air
with
its zero shine disguises, swinging

Paddle the not where belief
is
anything that is said
an
image successful shoots
first but answers few
questions police siren
whips
through a dream
betrayal mirrors drowning necessity,
oceans of breakables diving into simile
(thrilling
in the most obvious reversal

Logopoeia world in a stolen
book
its nodes glisten identity
which
is speech wind
which is voice image
which street flaked
out
puking guts audible
pool of blood above
the visible morality of the low
life –
invisible from the helicopter's mirage

Coming Down from St George's Hill

for John Muckle

1

Leaf-shield privacy the
Nervous system no longer
Uncollected air reels
Into a
History of human stability
Public notice coming down
From the hill
                it's like
Being invaded from within
Becoming parasites in a
Psychosomatic flounce
Of net with silken light
For a street of beggars
Dark milky way of useless
Jewels
Personalised
Initial possessions
With eviction panic
                    ditch
The child's bailiff's boot
Sinks fuel rage
Blocked
Truant at the crumbled mouth
Up to the master's lips
Mirror-bred seduction
Scales
Actualising stupor with
Silk tickling privacy
Cut
Through the triple glazing

2

Travelling time the way I had
Pushing back the little savings
Absorbed talk to the slaves
Options
For affirmative literature
Teaching erect income
Of property pert
Beneath her drapes housing police
In jellied waiting
                you don't
Exist at a commonsense level
The pain of suitable desire
Bites work is skimmed off
Behind the drapes the poem's
Scarlet exposures
Privilege their hot counsel
Our needs re-routing desire
Attempting open freezing
On the wet waiting list
Upstairs
In somebody else's
Purchase defining agendas
To court the plaintiff
Escapes
To the fringes of burnt out
Demolition laugh says Stephen crying
Mud deaths house us or micro-fascist
Victims trapped in
Dog discipline
The scream beyond the eviction wasps
The rotting apples they leave
Mine
The semantic fields

3

for John Holmes

Democratic vista he parks the car
Then has to queue for the cashpoint
Whispering possessive St George's
Somewhere above the embossed logo
Window tissue paper
And its history of pleasantly
Attired servants
In famous fables begun at this
Desk of irregular
Attic windows car door opens blonde
Hair spills into the gutter
He speaks in deadpan cockney learned
Of the East Sussex school of villainy
Creaming himself at Thatcher's rush of
Active citizens revving up
Fumes and consumption's vapour
Lists a pop capitalist
                           transformed
A staggering dislocation of the
Cocktail effect gone defective
Electric against meshed frost
Produced by desire dreams
An act of love a realised cell
Phone interrupts *you all right mate?*
Giggle at least it stopped a repetition
Of his ardent administered dream

His Furious Skip

You're no hypnotist as a beckoning
Finger sends a death squad to
Their senses   Skytrail from a
Military jet falls as sclerotic vertebra
Collapsed on his arms dreams of
A process in which balance
And tip are equals

Fill the structure and all hell breaks loose
Freebie rollerskated   Moves across
My empty place to kill it
The noise of rain like rice poured
Slowly onto a drum

Armoured cars lift the filthiest
Artifice   Of one system into another
For a symptom you manufacture

Persona fills the scarce dishes warped
In the head   Hopes that have been
Privatised in the silence

Cleanliness of their cutlery while the husbands

Measure their erotic logic   I watch
The child running and she slaps to the ground
In tears   Arousal files a literature where
The assassins rid us of prime doubts   That's
Desire off the table afraid to kick

Sudden sexless

Image of self misrecognising   Solids drip   She's
A little operator shaking cigarette packets

That others have left   One more
Trickle in the cleft of the spine shifts

Involuting cloud vibrating
Against some taut but invisible chairman's
Agenda   Creates a world cover process
Satellite dish aping the ape working

Politics of the next   Hasty executions
Where the iodine radiation is who
This information impacted

Strung along the bar   They're the invisible
Machine   Only disputed territory   Stumbled
Upon the cardboard colony   One sentence
Pressures the ecosystem   Dust of tea

The words 'eternal' and 'feminine' dancing

Buttocks on her keyboard fucking
A nonsense print out   Knows who has
Shares
Regressive beliefs   Out and up the blade
He clicked his fingers to bring

My own unlikely stereotype against

Anaemic detail   To choose the paleface Gothic
Your thoughts pushed back by the new machine

Meteors of scrape against this red door

Shit hits the door mat   Click he says
As the light goes on   This skill
Has no value   He produces
A falsely figural text of his phantasies
Non-voters are supporters
Under the unprofitable street-lamps

Flickering over their page foregrounds hyena
Party   Elsewhere in the system lenses
Flushed into the sewers focus these
Thoughts   Unwanted and silver
Commodity and rhythm   A hierarchy
Of needs is still a hierarchy

Sado-masochistic cross-gender
Management techniques   Am I speech
Hooting automata   Speed your wire
Into the speaker   In its silence

The terror of balancing in the unlit
Carriage   Burns   The spontaneity
Of Hofmann's ground   Vigilant
Black icing   Knifed but not ignored

You can't be ontological and still
Want pleasure   The real house
Is built by carnival   Turn your
Accountant sour   Eros
And Thanatos impose their iambics

Memory's thinking mind   It's bedtime
Bliss with the cupids   It's fur and
Pearls as well as sensible shoes   On
A public scale   Be a product
To preface it with   Fuck the machine from
Behind and it pumps out money

The shadow from multiple sources

Eyes a radical definition
Of personal space   To shove down their throats
The father of the brain-damaged boy plays
Tunes on your teeth

Dense oddities floating   Desire
Must compromise   I look at the
Cars and they crunch   Boy Scout
Anarchism   What to inject that won't
Bring bleach convulsions   Something we
Want mankind to be
Glances through the chickenwire   Functioning
Slits without eyes

Coins down the lavatory in the last half inch

Key off   Missing parts

Skytrails before dawn assert somebody else's
Vigil   Withholding information in
Fashion   Collect the forgotten
To insert in strange bathrooms   If forms overlap
How can they   Fade discourse slashes
Without history   The whole is non-situational

Knives and forks with almost a fleshly pleasure

Riskless wipes away doubt the news   Pink slips
Arranging   The stiff unfolding of a chequebook
TV lunch wheels in millions
Of untitled titles

Boy shouts to his father on the new office roof
On every hoarding an involuntary
System of ID   Patch that whistles over
A stop on the line   Who will recognise
Thought was to one side or not real
As she jumps out to his deepest deposit

Speaks to a man driving through fog
Fill in the space with your impacts   A
Satyr spray-guns cock and balls on a tree

Discipline from this head refracting   In the
Ecosystem   A hundred hours community service
Electronically stamped on his wrist

Three Poems by Wayne Pratt:
from *The Penguin Book of British Parrots*

Suez

As I gaze now at your curling photograph
Tucked into the corner of the chocolate box
Brimming with saccharine snaps,

I recall those holiday trees, stirring
As though tremulous fingers were
Searching the scalp for lice.

He gave me my first cigarette there
In exchange for my coveted condom
And I was sick before the discarded match

Had cooled. He shrank,
Embarrassed, boyish, the hangman's mask
Flopping to a squab.

The afflatus of history in the rabbit hutch:
Eden's picture covered with pellets.
'Guess who?' – soft girlish fingers pressed over my eyes.

I first saw the marbled skin of your thighs,
The silvered crutch of your discarded knickers,
As he kissed you (his sister) goodnight.

But the next day I refused to follow
The mouse-tracks into the lichen with him,
But stayed home to stroke the cat instead.

Fornication: Spoof on Quoof

Limp now, I turn away.
No longer can I face
The heaving spaghetti

Of your steaming sex, or
My elephant's fumblings
In the bamboo pit of our bed.

Hunching over your foetal back
On the infertile
Gulf of our marriage, I hug

My *hottie-wottie-boggie*
And say goodnight.
This childhood name

Brings back the muscular arms
Of my mother, hauling
The black-bottomed kettles

Onto our northern griddle,
Spanking the rubber flanks
Of the spouting hotties.

My only consolations now
Are these virile images
Tossed up in a spray of old words.

Against Paternity

Sniffing through my daughter's knickers
For traces of toxic glue
Brings back the joy of Airfix Spitfires,

Talismans of the heroic father
I never knew, invented for school-friends,
A square-jawed fiction to set against

The wreckage of reality: dead
In the Battle of Britain when terminal trails
Etched the sky like string.

The father whom I left behind was 'put away'
For offering sweets to little girls; my
Teddies lined the wall like Nuernberg judges.

His photo watched like a bleeding Christ
Above mother's catholic, all-embracing bed,
As I recalled the fate of the fathers' sins.

I can still hear her voice echoing down
The terrace, *'And don't come back ya bugga!'*
To each ephemeral figure tripping away on the cobbles.

Identifying 'him' (as we called him) in the mortuary,
I recall the expressionless unkissable lips
And his penis curled like a frozen prawn.

The Magnetic Letter

homage to Bob Cobbing for his 69th birthday

Each perfect dot means
just what it wants,
inking mimesis clean
off the putrid tang of summer
in the city. Your only escape is
to bend over backwards
into the echoing airshaft. Beasts
escaped from headlines, their
instincts caught in jagged wave-pulses
unspeakably human, sink
into a sewer speech bubbling
forever, boiled by the
brand names that sold us
us. Bulldozer welfare teams
roll out the dazzling marketable
vistas, detoxicants dumped
where the magnetic swarms
pick your luminous trees clean.

Melting Borders

Those buckets of blood there are the president's property;
they reek of recent history, but have nothing to do
with what has become your fault; leakages
of household gas that punch too-distant disaster-holes
in the indifferent sky. He'd skipped from jail to the
palace, rhyming with corpses that had fallen for him.
This is the first free bulletin for 40
years: his bullet-soaked face rolling
across the divisions of our suddenly parallel lives,
between striking ambulancemen and prisoners
handcuffed between 2 wall-charts: 'Given to Charity'
and 'Given to Shareholders'. Scab paramedics
give the *all clear* to the prostitutes' civic poses
in the glow from the ambulance windows,
after checking for small-scale social infections, now
8% of council tenants own shares. Why
these people come here, I don't know, great
gangs of lack of proof roaming across our lack of purpose.
One terminates every 2 seconds. Up
from the sewers, I will shoot into the celebrant crowd
until the fervent anthem of my machine gun
dies. I was a food-taster *and* sex-trap for him;
he took fingernails as hard currency. Violated orphans
like me are loyal to the people's secret brides:
old grain for sale in foreign-aid sacks, while you
worry about which gospel gives most truth,
where tangled colour-coded wires can be read
as misery-indices in 3-D; or where a pictogram of
a whale's tail dives into the charitable fund.

from Smokestack Lightning
a mythology of the blues

for Tony Parsons

Let it all go. As I sing I drive my
dynamite for some strange machine
of this nearly spent century;
the big city calls its sinful
numbers heaven. My fast rolling
kisses are for the stern
lady, dodging me, back of the beat.
Our harp player's dead – when Pete
told me, we laughed. A quick shimmy
was Elzadie's goodnight; buttons and
belt loosening, Arvella's swift farewell.
Pete's 12 string steam whistle leaves town;
I want you to take my place in this song.
Elzadie lifted her hem and smiled, as he
tuned to an open chord. Bending G on the E,
the dog jumped into the horn as
the KC moaned, with a mocking beauty
mating rabbit foot dreams. Arvella slumped in
the shade, feeling contempt, thinking: give me
the train's shake. Sweat rolled off
transport as delight, a nervous fix
in this thief's paradise of form and
necessity possessed by devils. He'd
rehearsed all morning, restless,
couldn't wait to start again, to howl
out, temporal and grounded, 'We'll never
get out of these blues alive' –
above the frets, trembling. Inside:
shared diction, dancing voices, mojo stomping,
good book palms together in prayer. At night
she wedges the chair against the door,
feels evil thrashing outside the room,

but can't connect the pose of his
arpeggio muscles above her, de-tuning
slackening; sings down the phone:
'Take my lonesome love in hand.'
Dancing with her to the juke band,
his tense fingers practise chord shapes
up and down her spine; to be a real person:
a girl adjusting her skirt, singing *Twentieth
Century Blues*, a pearl on her lips, –
her devil astride two chairs, playing slide
with a Coca-Cola bottle. She
is about to say something over the
gossamer telegraph line, to survive
his strong hands rambling through.

from Killing Boxes

Soil keeps you in touch
on a piece of somebody
else's shit still turning on
that word beautiful isn't beautiful
torn in two directions transit
van debates wait for the
sunset just a blob to
me the arab shadows reality

Faces in the crowd emerge
from the emergency a confidential
whisper in my ear desires
peacenik erections on charts showing
positive coverage, as libidinal victors
curl tongues inside her want –
less convincing mumbling involves the
spinning rhetoric cares for you

Nothing erotic in this writing
except the writing kissing her
tattooed shoulder, lifting champagne to
long-laid hellacious phallicism, rubber
tents and missiles melting, penetrating
the mind favourable images from
art a war running with
the movie rights just run

Sand spray as a tank
dips a word gorgeous as
condoms over the gun barrels
the successful sergeant's string
of gassed canvas the network
sings open the window veto

there is a riot panic
printed on the contradictory winds

Behind that Union Jack curtain
the terminal fire-fly armadas
run pure liquid diagrams more
launch law than pilots dream
windows of the street rumours
of explosions at somnambulant destinations
focus the single man singing
the news through broken teeth

Listening to the combat fashion
the theatre smoke drifts across
boys on the piazza listening
to hours of hissing leader
tape passing the heads of natural
outrage. They have been
used, selling smaller dredgings from
costlier sparkles on foreign rivers …

It's a lie. He rushed
off a blurred list of
names the mad laugh deep
from an insomnia that seemed
all surface sees during the
blackout of this news war
no voices lines crackling with
fleet laws for the sleeping

He's only one of many
postcards of cover shots the
rotorblades of smile in proper
poses of reason this night
is arrested and those bandages
will be collaged on those
vox pop cheering flash desk
men, recoding this masked desire

The sand's hot line burn:
wildcat smears under postmodern technologies,
t-shirts sporting these maps stretched
across camera thumbs-up, measuring
all manhood against princess warriors
in metal battle bras, jinking
oily luxury, dripping liberty under cover
of darkness or charred infernos

Our evidence for this? Wrecked
bent metal was shareholders' rig
dropping down tornado seed, war
pit monsters operatic talking heads
with smoke grained voices wild
weasel zap music as the
mother of instability crackles and
you hear the dream roasting

Fucking Time:
Six Songs for the Earl of Rochester

for Gavin Selerie

Dream of your eyes,
lips like leeches;
a wayward bullet invents
Fate as it

flies; worms twist his
armour; blood-scabs
on his prick. Appetite
leads, Aversion stands

off: peck and claw,
eye to eye.
She strokes fur; beauty
spots pock her.

Pissing fountains' vapour dances
before his milky
eyes, watery lids. A
million moments fuck

time, knotting the sequels
of pleasures, the
backdrop of fallen whores
and standing pricks.

'Phoebus tosses feeble shadows;
Nymphs spoil for
frolics. The first deflowered
blossoms the ~~brightest~~

(del.)

                    ~~briefest~~
    (*del.*)

                      barest

Power and powder; blanched
stone in sunlight,
dog turds in shadowed
ditches. Leather dildo

spies the clap-sick
passions. Mares frisk
at the royal carriage.
She becomes coinage

of the realm, false
'incorporeal body', brisk,
pregnant, a bladder of
policy, bursting shit.

Saw the print of
her shape in
the grass, led the
coranto around Mercury's

frauds or Jupiter's adulteries,
leaf-mould hoof
rings where satyrs fuck:
shutters, mid-stage.

She spreads her fan:
her pearl fingers
frig lords. She performs
his dowry snatches.

Twist the pressure of
external things void,
a turd stirring beneath
her gown, perfumed

lice crawling a woven
scalp, mechanical fingers
scratching a lap dog,
two bitches licking

one prick; running over
an alphabet to
start a rhyme, warring
'tarse' against 'arse'.

Breath steaming, his thigh
roasts at your
fire, lover's meat skewered
on butcher's eye.

Slap him like a
saddle, lewd engine!
Fat *bougre* in the
stocks, his neck

hangs like arse lard,
or fleshy backs
of old mistresses. A
beast, spitting sperm.

from Empty Diaries

Empty Diary 1903

What happened to
our chorus? We
blossomed in artificial
light, wasping at
the honey glow;
chanted in the
boudoir to wake
to conversations, falsely
witnessed, pasted upon
a depthless dawn.
Our hips on
his desk prevented
work; one breast
sacrificed yesterday to
the depths of
his contraption, pinned
above his throne.
This sovereign of
his own name
fades with each
retelling, belongs to
none, mortal for
the first time
in history, feels
the remains of
gatling gun passions –
our delightful losses
lost in lyric.

Empty Diary 1905

She falls for him, conventional longing well
tutored, no pose held, broken but breathing,
yet she keeps a finger in a
page of last year's tightly scribbled diary:
the ranked delights of the Paris corsetière,
the dummies' impersonal whorish display of lace
and china flesh, a flat-buttoned pressing
of chambermaids' etiquette; I can't bear his
'I sleep, I wake, I never dream'
; want to slit his throat, to hoist
him, dripping from his penis; her story
stalled, veins in her bare neck pleading.

Empty Diary 1926

for John Seed

We push cars on their sides, jeering
them out

          coal lorries with police guards
smoulder outside the depot's gates and

nervous clerks in tin hats salute débutantes
peeling spuds with bloodless fingers:

history's tight membrane

the age's leaking sewer,

revolution, spirits one broken machine gun in
a pram

hold out

until the police clear the Broadway for
the British Gazette

for one instant

Baldwin's hanged and we call this

Love

Empty Diary 1936: The Proletarian News

for Charles Madge

vauxhall was grey she needed blocks of
flats not jewel panopticans she threw back
her hem and did a tight city
fling tyrannical wireless valves on tulip faces

echoes of men patronising answers on folded
blankets heads bubbling with pints of stout
rotten teeth of her voices skin always
gleaming an unblemished marching announcing sore lips

surrealist commodes adorn the scattered floors of
chaotic meal times in houses of the
poor dash of belisha peril in jitters
waiting for the paraffin fire to blow

Empty Diary 1946

I ration my eyes on a Demob
suit, zip up the lids; winter boots.
The immodest mermaid flexes on his useless
muscle, her flesh his loaned oily skin.

I'm beached on his dream, a nostalgic
pillow of breasts pulled tight, a War:
a mission fulfilled that leaves him marching.
Steam brushed love from the platform farewell.

I turn from him, in judgement, breathing
his regret. He stomps the wrong side
of a pre-War newsreel; a rally. His
eyes bore into my back like bullets.

Empty Diary 1954

We are statues of ourselves, stiffened eulogies
in the arthritic history of imperial endeavour
(the world of his syllabics: the words
we silently mouth: our faces networks of

electric lies: our lips would seal: our
eyes close on a world which will
drill its electrodes into our mermaid flesh
sketched in by the boss) Say it:

We lick the pellicle of your absence,
Nazi leather stitching your bulging zip (*stilyagi*
skinny kids shivering outside the wimbledon palais
filter sin through newsprint skin us alive

Empty Diary 1955

Office blocks imagine lift shafts for themselves
but offer slatted stairs. Neat masking tape
paths square the lawns. The plate glass
fades the girls from their adding machines

under a slice of you and your
approaching world: a crystal defect swimming its
buckled skin. His syllabics rattle your timely
heels: gooseflesh rises along your attempt at

ease
      (listen, that's *desilu* laughter canned in
history's back row)
                You trip up slippery
steps to appointment you shake his confident
fist: smile at his unscheduled rubber horns.

Empty Diary 1967

*As I entered
her*, I knew
that her chosen
posture would be
silhouetted against a
thousand bedsit walls;
a revolutionary posing
as sex goddess
well into the
twilight of such
idols; alone with
his voice between
the shelves of
Better Books ('I

am a Sadist!')
fixing it, *a*
transparent hero glued
to this vinyl
table top!
             before
she broke me
like a statue,
history sacked by
super heroines boiling
mundane flesh, leaving
not one drop
of fat for
the police to
scrape up: *Utopia!*

Empty Diary 1968

'For the man who
           has me...'
her eloquent slips black
           my discourse,
this second skin, or
           so she's
been told by her
           second mind.
My tattoo sweats her
           name. She
enters me on a
           useless giggle,
then squats at the
           master controls,
punching slogans into consciousnesses
           sweetened for
rotting the fangs of

>   *Capital.* I
> wrote her onto the
> pillow, a
> hot boy pressing for
> a kiss,
> his Anti-Universe, sunrise from
> her bathrobe;
> Or: truncheoned jeers, diesel
> coughs, she's
> manhandled into the gaping
> Black Maria.

Empty Diary 1974

City's dead weight trenches the subject
down, beneath her sensible blouse. Eyeliner

Asserts squatters' rights on her gaze;
fear pins her up onto her

Stark mesh of blemishes. 'I'm lost
and I'm late – in equal proportions.'

She has the money in used
notes, her life in soiled narratives,

As his pristine story would tell.
The ladder of his enquiry leans

In a director's peep; her supposed
firecracker passions leave sex toys for

His subjectivity to play with. Says:
'The police cleaned up Utopia forever.'

Empty Diary 1982: I Tiresias, You Jane

for Peter Middleton

'At the bed's
edge she mirrors
her clitoris, *her*
fuse; the eulogy
to translucent flesh
inscribes desire on
"her menstrual bloat".
She's waiting for
a powdery man
who won't faint
at the sight
of her blood'
(*HER NAPALM HAIRDOS*

'Beyond the mirror
he tries not
to watch, to
sniff out kindness,
to find the
lexis that leaves
no flattering lick
across my belly.'

'His body wasn't
built to be
looked at,' *I
think,* 'terror's statue
unveiled in private.'
His umbrella drips
in the corner.

Empty Diary 1987

i.m. Félix Guattari

Empowered image Baudrillard
framed by one
new Duchamp urinal
per second dolly-
oracular heroes hammering
MASS-MEDIATING CHAOSMOS
she's 'voice' trickling
her absence subverting
the flow of
dominant redundancies paste
book sticky life
worlds vending mermaid
flesh art-thick
fresh referents sing
for lyric shifts
in subjectivity spilling
sky (the hour
glass gravity of
articulate slaves: *she's*
beautiful on the
executive bed, existential
territory. *He's* cut
to the balls
at the kitchen
sink, subjective autonomist,
fucks alone within
you, tasteless sucker
of silicone flesh

Empty Diary 1990

Past empty rooms full of men, the
street's alsatian ears pricking up, she searches
for evidence of kindness, but finds annotations
blowing her apart into whatever use her
senses and limbs can make of them.
The smiling professions ease her into loss,
with embalmers' soft assurances, each migratory text
striving to be total. Her lips, pursed,
mouth a public language to parade in.
An alien resident of delirium, adrift in
dialogue, the arguments small but binding, she
lives in voices that aren't hers: *Anything
else*? (Capital's plea.) Pit bulls sniff their
masters' tattoos, as rusted muscles melt in
percussive light. She recalls late capitalism, its
vascular delights. Dogs bark liminal threats to
its exchanges; bland ugliness, it's never enough.
Her voice, stuck in the ventriloquist's gullet,
uses what she finds, takes what she
can use: 'There're too many eyes here,
running on empty, too many faces whipping
posts of prohibition. These people too easily
file somebody else's history, their own shadows
jumping out across windscreens to greet them

from The Lores

Book 1: Time Capsule

The time capsule's
contract with the
future, the Eugenics'
Court with its
injections, co-ops us
to a selective
history: as soon
as the population
is trafficking clatters
the shutters down
the laws of
motion beyond its
jurisdiction, unceased husks
in lightning streaks

Flicks to see
who flinches empty
me from your
circumference, accommodations of
space an abacus
for millions who
stand beside us
pure result with
no contest empty
microphones and dead
amplifiers inside each
rule if she
moves any slower
she's our commodity

Untitled epics re-tell
the saga in

technicolor prose, translation
of the corporeal
substance into utopian
glitter where the
public stands and
the people rush
by eyes like
drains (*the plenitude*
I generate, broadcasts
never made) at
each street corner
gather unregenerate genes

Sequencing witness the
world is his
phenomenology of caprice
lets the barbarians
through the breach
family values juiced
on marble his
deliberate misreading of
the signs to
reach the other
side of them
courts opacity's bride –
the hiss of
consciousness accompanies each

Not his penis
as a message,
deeply, which she
must groan, splits
down the phone
a surplus night
of cocktail eyes
for the skin
is where war

is experienced. He
plays veins under
folded sheets   government
building   towers of
voice   incorporated ethics

She's been crying
as she voted
buying in hyperrealities
saline fear dripped
in her jumpy
heart passing an
Elder hanging from
a lamp post
this past week
Our particularity is
our universality (I
shall not dig
into the weak
loam of conscience;

the issue is
that we acted
without reflection, without
remorse, scripted from
the outside, black
posters limpet to
the face of
substance eyes which
could stare through
bars at the
Tomb of the
Unknown Dictator) iced
lust after our
video tape snags

The electrolysis of
Reason gold that
gathers a glint
a light seed
too brilliant to
penetrate from the
Brutal Streets to
The Forest Way
wasted promised land
the cut telegraph
in univocal complicity
an oscillation of
the *geist*, dimmer
switches on passion

Under the portcullis,
departmental seal, minister's
strategic reinvention a
constantly repeated assertion
in my life
the usual call
signs that announce
the world's messages
back-announce interventions
incidentally sliding into
incidents, notes found
on cyanide corpses
the grand narratives
in encapsulated form

To find the
broken melodies of
a world humming
to him alone,
wordless traffic burns
viral headlines tremble
in his lap

questions bolted through
skin balanced on
a beam they'll
be kicked from,
noosed (Unceased, in
another book, just
guns already smoking

Book 9: Torn Elegy

for Lawrence Upton

primed with sand outside the bars
decrees token-legislate girls lugging buckets
across the public will adores it
free fists raised revolution never imminent
potentially positioned behind each final portrait

his interventionist mug-shot burdened with
conquered streets each glint of red
for his final surrealist grief their
sneering revolution aggressive and cosy they
invite him in fragrant as death

slammed shut in existing conditions newsreels
behind Franco's sandbags feel good they
enter the old clause of nothing –
no white flags no enterprise basements
falangist dolls take the pluming town

negotiate steps with calculated terror shed
his grief peppery stone virgins safe
in neologism logistics the final frontier –
sweat slides so far from blood
and sperm unloaded pistol going off

unlock our atrocity arsenal grief barricades –
corpses curl around dying horses the
name is Europe the smile behind
each proper victim vacates whistles and
tracks the space across prepared lists

affirmative concepts cut their muddy throats
poetics of impact scarce proper nouns
whose faces flesh radio banners tape
follows the track of stress (plots
collapse on the way to consensus

futurity salutes from fur the spoils
trawl her torn flesh wires a
cough patched up territory spitting debris –
too many witch wireless altars turn
out to be virgin boot sermons

weep the humming of rapturous release
beds shaded with belligerence beg
cigarettes unconscious communism delirious feet in
gutters sheltered by blood, our deft
shifts of weight as we witness

law surrendered pockets stuffed with challenge
scramble heavenward clawing grenades taught that
they owned the voice trawling each
waveband sensation bonded weight in commitment –
little utopic slogans become each chill

delete the struggle diaries wiped out
beliefs the fruit of nobody loiters:
even the reprisals of these vigorous
tenders, potential gifts beneath torn elegies –
(as returning priests swell Madrid, *adorned*

sculpt with corpses revolution's confused transistor
voices call him back from peep

holes shelled through dwelling and sensory
prolapse, selfish searches for shifting hope –
torn fences flutter with price tags

laced sleeves falangist realism at half
mast provisional monuments a multisystemic screeching
against a contract of brittle orchards
cannot be contracted from aprons leading
dispositions to blackshirts with intelligent limbs

collisions regulate resistant refrains gutter muscles
link the anguished knuckles a taste
censor's glance spits scraps to negotiate
with futurity, to strip the mummified
nuns, to worship their fossil mortality

not afraid of refutations permanently contingent
on *campesino* encounters miners' women fit
facts into prison clothes insurgent dust –
their shoulders shake bloodthirsty tongues behind
poetic sash windows passional full stop

Book 10: Pumps Primed with Fire

Fanatical beings refunction the banners
driven to exchange ritual policies
what's inside you quiet embattled
slices bricks with quixotic custom
and practice against slogans, a
thingy day in the nervy
90s the new erotics underfoot

With homemade worlds less administered
taken from dream bolts and
no splinter groups of wounded

fabulists no heart or pocket
to speak with predictable phatics.
You want to turn banknotes
clean? *it's a free country*

Magical splices he roars power
cuts deep removals from utterance
roving prince of fury pursued
by our shouts: sherry glasses
tremble in knuckled Piccadilly club
the spectator's hand repockets dodges
in a corporeal adjustment ingrained

Antibodies to unreason impressions give
up the abandoned tune in
her voice micro-slogans positioned forever
behind shaky unofficialdoms hand held
edits shudder ethics (cleansing pose
each choice for collocation; vibrant
illusions of our sore feet

Cascades wing the loves a
speculation they starve the gape
in a network of interferences
an anti-monument of buried disguise
a helicopter circles missiles fixed
hardens the negotiable fudge the
brutal poise and clipped voice

Phrase fashion positioned henceforth on
dark symbolic streets lines aflame
whisper crackling radios Yes-hostages
perceptions complicit with each green
and black flag decommissioned consultants
sing the way they've been
reported, pumps primed with fire

Bombardment flicks the day back
on its lores your rôles
up to speed razor your
stare territory losing trade secrets –
multiple spaces patch the last
Sindicato contract fiercely imminent for
each next generation's conquered streets

Scan your spectre legitimising banner
proud scratch artists still alive
horny antennae in the back
streets recite their manifestoes in
Crusoe roof gardens (as we
make the links, lines of
the many turn the name

The Last Muggletonian catches it
frames Cable St resistance out
for communitarian hand-shackles escorted
diversions amid machines for living
rub themselves watching some battered
authority left in decline (corporeal
human resource at the margins

Disposal, each sense ambient: microphones
simply there launch politicians in
precautionary sell-outs, anodyne risk-
antidotes, Trafalgar duties of the
chained bunting for a Labour
victory. English lyrics spread the
linen, sterile or not; corporate ethics

Invite heroines' effluvia your noisy
transfer your contract knowledge which
has itself become scaffolding enactments
of respect: judgement shines on
paving stones faculty without shudders

the fierce navigation of nomadic
ethics, loathing lacy discourse silhouettes

Adjustments ingrained for life, the
agonistic ritualists chant everlasting exchange
consultation as a waistcoat turns
in self-confirmation: appetites lead
one banner reaches the daily
script: the pitfall scars of
the delegate modulate the lores

History or Sleep

> *And we are allowed to be happy*
> *sometimes. Indeed it is our duty.*
> Anthony Rudolf

Less real than a dream
logged in
archaeologists' ledgers
propels awareness
along another axis
hangs a veiled
filter for your presence
a gauze a
gaze figures inward
dirtying cuffs on the world
wraps the teeming air
in chalk upon a wall
a voice-activated
future on the blink
surrounded by threats
a new point of view
refugee witness's
shallow relief
slapping into the silent hallway
herself
on her television
at the fingertips
bigger suits work out
the countryside
its collapse ratios
the people
real news from virtual
travel
stretches
through force; cold defence
in these narratives as
obliterated landscapes

He wants to be watched the
events the camera
misses notate
the little utopias to
turn them to song (almost)
impassive but knowing
eyes
drink the swimming
passion, pleasure's
measures
beating sunsets each
wall a collision
a vaporous gleam
a sinking body he examines
pleasures
herself rolls across the floor
at a pinch a pluck a
spoor knuckling
happy sometimes, hardly seems
our duty to brush
with the palm
moving
in such a way
sets this in motion so
he enacts
the bye-lores
unscheduled
she pulls him into
the pool of her
watching
pushing aside
each scheduled routine
horror

One raped
can another relax

stroke
orgasmic dead fur
from this catalogue of
terror, frog-eyed navigators
chart us
while enemies invade
(liberate) equivocal
loyalty
tells us we cannot afford
to open the window
you cannot see
another's sorrow without
hanging
on the breeze, a counter
to think and feel
pleasure empty
as a mouth willing cool
scarecrows itself
replaces
all with its fevered dreams
of possible tomorrows
bark
you wake (your victim
pours from you
virtual memories conflate
occasions
dissolve
salt sweat stains
to find – who? – dead)
the recognition that
another human being has responded

haunts

Jumping out of the groove
of an ancient technology

through a smashed hole
in the reflection of a dead sky
no epicentre
to this crowd
in your front garden
selling marked-up beer
WHO KILLED JOY
a cheesecake smile
changes the standard
endlessly
to the shape of the advertised map
paying to gawp at it
zigzags around the body
a hand upon your shoulder
in proprietorial embrace
you act out your life
the faulty vending machine
twitches

Left enough spoors
in the gold zone
for others to pick up the trail
in the third
person's silent grip
at the edge
of memory myself
steady as a leaf
)identity
enclave(
his old anecdote wove
another lie, another life
through
obliterated place names through
tangles
(recounting

The ceasefire never
declared you will
be menaced
to contribute to the
hunger striker tattoos
under her sleeve in affront
surfaced quotas
a window
locked in re-enactment
to be a classic reference in
the mouth of a displaced proletarian
slept
for itself dreaming
of the Fenian submarine
a stone on a hot beach echoing
plausible twists into
actuality
a household name in
whose houses around
the polluted brilliance of
the omphalos

He no longer burns
startlingly bright in this post-'79
dispersal he
sweats into song beholds
the sprinkled mountains of Poland
affliction at the gate
diaspora on your
doorstep
the town had been
cleansed
stone patriots escaping
into the grain
of his table top sheen
wings sticky with pollen

turn green with fear
amid leaves
as the kestrel
turns
favoured media ejaculation
teaching the peacock to sing
policed dreams
accusations
arcane rules
arsonists' kindlers
murderers' armourers
the president's map
on the back of a banker's draft
obliterates
air space
'on the ground'
there are snapshots of tears
escaping
at the wheels
lucky bandages
desert tygers
striping the sand with fear
a world
rapidly unreacting

A mask tricks its wearer
bearer
wherever the body
escapes each queen bee needs
workers to lift her costume off
shivers flesh down a dancing thigh
can constitute no mind
for this gathering
dispersal
needs no people: they
need no reminding

vapour of their own shit
vents in Victorian manhole covers
he's upside down the
crisp bursts of his micropower
but there's nothing to say
we wanted the world
and we wanted
it then
in its invasion
of the ordinary with spectacle
in their labour
radiates joy
carnival's flesh given over,
not up; a can kicks itself
along the street
the way she
touches
a door slams in Hindi
masks the oily faces
finding themselves dancing for a crowd
nice handcuffs on the right
to remain silent

To be happy sometimes
to let pleasure drift as
soon as you see the
enemy start shooting you
owe it to yourself to
pleasure
build
demolish
the honeysuckle bricks while the
cement blows free
delineations of pure joy
liminal numbness
between sleep and

objective market forces
stockpiling new stone on the periphery
around Being's crumbled Shack

You you
monadic resemblance light of
the world re-enacted as
retinal shimmer, its own
stink in its nostrils: I smelt
you long before I met you, she
says to the stiff, dripping
merman, sinking
in pleasure, who discovers her
gash of flesh
unzips her gown he licks each breast
as she watches, smiling
she kneads his submarine
body slips through
her fingers could he suck
her final gasp
she flushes him with
pleasure pricks
his tongue desperately happy
cannot fill her she
hoists him in
pleasures pleasure
hieratic annihilation
feeds off their shoulders

Bags outside charity shops
rifled by
women you've never seen before
blitz emanations
pushing antique prams
diaspora

from visibility
bones surrounded by pots
polluted sunshine
invisible smog spitting
on the chained gladiator
re-enacting one hour
of this street
sucks his face set
against the *axis
mundi*: a self, a
legionnaire
stranded on the
edge of Empire's
mosaic dice
checking identity papers
incendiary attacks
on overflowing rubbish bins
scorch the moths
not dusted from maps
bricks scaled to hands
body auras
cleansed
in reformation
the queen of consumer affairs
building to rubble, to
saleable brick, a new point
of view in next week's mausoleum

Camels kick
ragged turf
under a brooding sky
dressed in white
for wisdom men
devolved
bells chime as they lift
reflections safe

in the palms
of managed lack
a feather snaps in the
multinational cast off
scrambling for
old light bulbs
drugged eyes mask
padded
in brass she sways up
to the hips
for the boys
in shades
claps around the circle
detonate passion
they disorder
the world to pattern themselves
for the pointing girl
embroidered
her own seduction
at her breathing beads
his body's marked
with safety pins
a satellite dish away
dancing on the slipway
ostrich feathers
key-rings
rusted
he flirts
gauging the impossibility
of everyday winds
whistling through
her brazen plaits
float
in his mirror eyes
on the back of his Honda
at the edge of his
conscious peep through

the curtains of more than
one country
blossoms on
his spirits
like freedom
pointing backwards
the girl chooses
his sharp kohl lips
in exclusion
upside down and plastic
the toy gun swings
from his shoulder

Talk transports
this dirty corner
a train a
rumour of its timetable
crashes
in asks the advert of itself
the track to the furnace
your edge of history
or sleep within this
trap you act
wings sticky
caught in summer's shade
pain correctly
centres this ecstasy
with humans
flailing and
flaring in dust

Three Hundred Word Sonnets

from The Lores, Book 8

no negotiations

tart! he shouts at the slot machine
armed to the teeth with retributive spite
erect on the plinth of his own mottoes
his gun-oily digits target our lips

a composite hero squanders his rationed milk
ghosts, nazis, saints, all alive at once
a smudge of human interest disrupts
this urban pastoral with a moment's self

it rubs itself watches another walk bare
buttocked across the room limbs improvise upon
a melody of clefts between tense shoulder-
blades, sharp breath ecstasies their communicative ethic

in times of black maps imagination is
intervention (zero hour malevolence trades in history

from Entries: Empty Diary 1996

for Jo Blowers

codes unrobed

tongue shooting pained bursts I'm as tall
as me on labels he sticks over
my fingers pussyfooting defiance ices my slaughter-
hole for his glans female scopophiliac rehydrated

gristle pictures in the body hidden from
my gaze as orgasm exits my face
shaves anxiety quivering his eyelashes with my
teeth *all eyes on his adjusted pouch*

frictionless richness with a perfect stranger a
flesh vessel that sinks us to shiver
as it's filled (anonymity cracks *yes please*

a pair of Fuck Me Shoes his
oily runnels unruly member he pulls back
the foreskin as though he is selling

Small Voice

for Scott Thurston

darkness drags

a headlight's irradiated cone fading to an
English print of shredded lane rheumy vapours
tickling in time the throat catches on
slices of transitory purpose lost in decline

watch a row of identical open trucks
head somewhere archaic like a Midland colliery
not singing praises it's not even singing
the sharp rasp rustles in the ear

a redundant germ that drifts this Age
of Irony now happening to be forged
it barely sustains its volume of displacement
the vandals have fled   the gate bangs

scoop phlegmy lyric from the clogging drone
from the rusted hinges' lament

bitter croak

The Push Up Combat Bikini: Empty Diary 2000

Such turned out to be the eternity the poet promised me, the bastard
Angela Carter

You're coming over all female.
Your conceit's too clean. Out
of the push up they're a let down,
deposits that won't quite register,
banked on your looking. You sniff
eroticism off dirty shifts, smudges of pelt.
I slip an ought, drop a stitch or two.
Hot gushes signal your retreat. Every
time I open my mouth out comes
a manifesto of a new literary movement!
Was that a poem, curling round you,
your nerves ajangle at syntax's opening?
It takes me and takes me
for somebody else, as you
push me out between its lines.
What might a poem be, elsed?
You dunk your aching, lived-in balls in ink
and roll them across the page.
I'm your shagged out Muse.
Take me over you this last time.
Whisper me Pearl, whistle me off.
I'll be a big register on your retina,
breathlessly weaving love for a puppet prick
that can be choreographed. I'm
pegged on that line to George's stuff
and nonsense. 'I'm only an instance of a fuck
fucking (he says (she says (*who says?*
The ventriloquist tongues my clitoris and it speaks.

(dedicated to the memory of Barry MacSweeney)

A Voice Without

To say and not say at
the same time, or

at a different time to not
say and yet say –

eversaying, yes-
saying, gainsaying,

truthsaying, lying,
neversaying so that it

closes into what has been
said; to say that I

am not saying, to not
say that I am not

saying, or at a
different time to say that

has been said, but *this*
will never be said, quite

simply, quite inexplicably,
has never been nor gone,

has arrived without arriving
at what has been, has left

without leaving what is known,
disappears into the unknown

which is left behind, as
never before, said.

Only the Eyes are Left

for Mina Loy

What coils under this raw
Sky is pain

Her blind stone eye possessed
By the filth

To which it holds
Faith

In her grandmother's stays
Girling

Felicity if only looks
Could cure virginity

Only the eyes the dust of
Stars clogging

The celestial chamber the
Bowery the café du néant

She grips the sides of the
Capsizing real in a

Manhattan
Apartment made of

Refuse in a grand refusal she
Makes him reel

Colossal pussyfooter
With lunar junk

Parody and Pastoral

a text or commentary for Veronica Forrest-Thomson

They may not be clever
creatures but they leave us
to iron sensation melted
on a deadly breeze

Rough beasts and rough
boys both relieve us, unloved;
we pay up responsible
for what they call themselves

Invade another language
to be invaded by it:
the burglar alarm
perforates the morning's shell

They stitch up our loves
our lives to a violation that
believes inviolate dwelling
open like all ears

Wails as a headache a
screen of pain that the
window flashes
in migraine streaks

Door slams then ignition coughs
up to voice our twinned words
entwined
where barbed wire bleeds

from Reading *The Reader* of Bernhard Schlink

This is not guilt but grief

From now on she will be in quotation marks

She emptied herself out with good reason

He is left empty for no reason good or ill. Reading

her absence as a presence he bears witness

His testimony is as blank as an orphan's. His testament is frozen sweat in solid steam…

A splinter of light in the eye. The illegible lines on her face as she turns to dissolve in your tears. Her eyes witness us. Witnesses on trial. The trail of testimony leads to our locked doors…

This is the Autobiography of a Dead Man. He feverishly entered history through her body. And died there. He buries the flower of his youth. He stands on his own grave as its memorial. During each night he is daubed with a swastika that he spends his days bleaching.

Call his body a work of art. Its story the catalogue. But telling the story is the same as not telling. Forgetting is louder than memory. Recall the half erasures guiltier than confession. Page upon page of the re-unrecalled. She built herself around him and he's on loan to her bare walls. She leaves him on show. (Who will believe him as the boy in the bad film of his ex-wife's memoirs?)

Her function is automated. His ticket has expired. The route is the margin between inquisitiveness and inquisition. A routine quiz.

Caught in the astonished archive   The past has passed   The present In a court of its own   Only the dead may represent themselves   Accused or abused   To embark anew   Test history's pulse   Only when it is stone will it move

Record A reflex beneath the throat. Waiting on its whisper

A writer is a reader re-incarnate

He censors his moment. The Disappeared of his own *Entartete Kunst*. Victims of his familiar venom. Between the lines lie many stories of abuse *Pause*

He is possessed of perfect recall but the lyre makes free with his story *Unpause* 'The suitors arrive each day for a decade. The uncalled call. Calypso listens at her own bedside. The odyssey of sleepwalk leads to the final dissolution of the lovers *Stop Rewind*

Play Never re-unworded. History has learnt to read itself

Legible scribbles on the pavement. Dribbles from the window-cleaner's bucket. The failure of the unilliterate

He is the dummy on Tradition's knee. The already spoken

A token

For the unsayings. A jammed broadcast East. Glossolalia on the instalment plan. The judge imposes a destruction order

Upon his words. Piled high like bleached bones in the unmuseum.

The reader is an inmate. Not an intimate. Unentitled. He re-inflicts her love-punishment. Upon himself. He breaks copyright. Transmits 'literature'. Perec's decent inverted commas. To her 'retrieval system'. To quote the Law. Her archive of torn throats.
        Commentary on a text is a decoy.

His nose is summoned. To sniff her out. Nuzzle the folds of the past. He doesn't believe the words his eyes show him. This is her place. She is an ear. Listening out for the dead. He is in love. With the sound of his own voice. She wants it in a little box. For undeportation. At least. She's in his hands. At last. But not in his arms. This is a taste of freedom. She could be released from his mouth. A curse.

He unpicks his brains. Unless he had sucked pleasure from the guilt. A child eats a tangerine first delivery post-War. The stomach of the cannibal god convulses. Twitches around them in ulcerous enclosure. He arranges this space. Nazi furniture. He reads her voice. Wipes the tapes.

Could not be allowed to return from where she had been. Should not read her among the dropped utensils. Her library of Holocaust Studies.

History stretched on its slab. Sickly with youth. Gets up. Walks off. Lets him climb. On the marble a monument. To his own silence…

Of the other stories. That didn't escape. Other readings. That did not want to get read. Speaking the written down will never recover the voice. An Audiobook of the Dead. For the long drive East. Recovery. And recovering. Scratch the loose earth covering the grave. On or off the record. Unrecovered. We are his responsibility. For ever

National Security, Huyton 1940

for Hugo Dachinger

Behind the eating huts of
Tent Village, vitamins

self-propagate while furred
rows of men nest in straw,

or cowled in gossip, whisper
down the fragile line.

Walled in a lost city, spotlight-
crazy-moons stutter

their aperture: centuries
of gazing focus

on escapologist smears at the
perimeter fence

flawed with fleshless nudes
free of barbed wire deletions.

Rail-tracks stretch to a watch-
tower dead under storm-clouds

billowed onto a tall sky of
taller stories, yellow with

optimism, read by filthed men.
He's sealed in the swart hut

thorned by telegraph pain, by
tangled sentries of wire-nest props.

He chalks a shiver of dusk
across their blackening list.

Three Figures Climb

Three figures climb
To freedom manacles cut

From walls but still weighted at
Ankles

Hoisted by the hero
Towards shadowy militiamen

Who carry axes unfurl
Unreadable banners

Below men too weak to
Move smell

The nauseous richness of freedom
A single torch in

Hollow darkness is enough
A proclamation

Fisted into their
Side of the bargain

A traitor's scab –
Dispersed in its own hush

The crowd catches the last cool word
Pillowed on congealing silence

Erotic Elegy

After Sigismunds Vidbergs' 'Revolution' (1925)

You thrash open the thick
Curtain interrupted we see

The troops bayonets
Fixed for entry they howl

For your sacks of gold
I moan for your reserves

Of desire both buried
I pillow against your breasts

Plumped in my shift
Brutal daylight

Shafts the length of my smooth
Legs from cool thigh

To bejewelled heel as I
Touch your arm I feel

You're ready to split and
Spill but we tremble as one

Providential storks on
The drapery shake

A pane crashes somewhere
I know they'll crack open

My curves like a shell
They're weak with war my

Enriched lips captive on
Your captured plush will

Offer full account in
The speech of the Phoenix

That now I see is what smoulders
Upon the auspicious drape

Prison Camp Violin, Riga

A brittle fiddle someone
Turns this on a lathe

Of the spheres where
Replica becomes the real

Thing thin
Birch treated knocked up

Catches an unhuman
Voice in its hollow

Thumbs moulded to pegs
Skewered into splitting holes

Tune the stolen wires a
Mollusc curled at neck's end

Fingernails
Pluck the kinked tune free

Out of itself a
Collapsed bridge

Sabotaged by
Time mittens

Grapple
The soup-bone bow-grip

Horse hair human
Hair taut straight like a well

Brushed bride's
Bends the tamed twig

Tucked under your chin the violin
Splinters against your jaw

As you draw the grinty
Voice out from the mechanics

Of survival: extinct
Livonian love song

from **Berlin Bursts**

Looking Thru' a Hole in the Wall

               don't
Destroy history spirited

Into the tainted air remains as
Its remains

Derelict monument to extra-human
Scale on sale as Pirate

Art gritting gritted
Teeth, mood

Recognitions across vacant
Division   balancing the hollow

Cusp of the wall a single
Book fans its open pages out

Of range of binoculars
Glass coffin temples &

Ghettos De Luxe –
Film escapades point

To posterity the shell of the
East & its visionary balconies

Out of Range

Sputnik on a stem
A boulevard of saluting

Tanks the unsecret head-
Quarters of the police ranked

Sweet jars
Of sweaty sex-swabs crazed

Dogs randy on the stink snap
At loins squeezed at gun

Point from worm holes a gift
Culture of the *nomenklatura*

The sheathed
Pleasures of ceremonial

Swords trumped up awards
Bookend Lenins &

Honnekers the dark stain
Of Directorate walls a narrow

Bed for the ultimate
Sacrifice squat telephones

Kept in the
Dark a bulky reel

To reel rolls out of an
Empty cocktail cabinet

Guarded gossip swivels
In ersatz

Modernity the
Reels spinning clacking

Spools a worthless archive
Of whispers

Sachsenhausen

1

Photographs of dogs guard the
House prices the dead

Make quiet neighbours he follows
The pilgrimage flapping in

White suit pursuit ponder the
Death March he catches

His breath his captive
Echoes repeated witness of a

Cover-cost testimony forever
Under the *Arbeit*

2

Watchtowers constrict the
Horizon granite slabs

Polyp'd with pebbles bodies
Tipped

From carts down basement chute no
Body speaks tiled room *preserved*

In shivering chill of doctors
Too scared to descend

To select tattoos on
Backs for science born

In guts outnumbered
By silence fresh

On the marble slab runnels
And sluices for human

Blood nobody looks in another's
Eyes colour

Coded receptacles for
Variegated garbage the

Clump of hair ghosting
A scalp

3

Wasp tormented rubbish bin a
Mausoleum of Coke cans that

A woman photographs a
Museum of extermination

Vitrines of stars nobody
Speaks to cover the ground

Crumbling splinters the Gestapo's
Green Casino abandoned

Strapline of hope *Mach
Frei* entering here the

Murmuring memorials over
The haunted shifting sub-soil

from Warrant Error

Immensity's blade rushes the wind and
grieves a full deck of bad luck

A managed democracy dances in tune
to a spread-cleft litany, as the Queen's English
warbler, toned to death, unstrews his truth

The blind justice hangs his slogan. Stop.
Burgeon a burden for the chant laureate
entuning and consuming his own genius. The comedy
terrorist brags his mince as roast beef

No peace fries up on a multiple mind grill,
dithering states in desperate times: the sandy
trap-door promise of paradise rusted by frost.
The biggest part of self weakens its softest
option: its cast out old iron alibi song

Steam from the nostrils of the talking engine,
Nervous sweat, stain your place in history.
I myself believe no matter anti-voiced

A crowd's pellicle riddled with restraint as
bulldozers cut deep veins in the sand.
Veiled bodies are piled in, no happy hour for
a last prayer, no compensatory *homaranismo*

I'll buy it, the testimony of the dead, the
imageless human cost: dark stars aloft
and dirty bombs below. I pay with portions
of myself billed in flickering slices. Gifting
the price, a real pain I say: 'As

soon as I write I I am gone (I am not) I
say (to 'my' self): "*Make yourself scarce*

Whose body crackles with self-quotation, tape-
loop requiem to which it loosens its step?

Your own secret department shuffles your
script, an Unconscious as collective as
responsibility. Or guilt. It's drift. No sifted
evidence while group-think shifts to shafting

Enough! Statutes selve up the sovereign
vote of little appeal, tagging new
lags, to purify the tribunals of the tribe!

Sense a Bright's light relief now an animated chip
of multi-kulti mufti moons across Baghdad as
rapid-eye as a dream of prime-ministerial photo-op:
a fantail of microphones lays his fantastic egg, and
blitzed martyr-bits pile up in paradise, next door

March 10

Burn friendlies on the wreck of human
terror the body of the people O!
Erato! scorched by the blaze of blue-on-blue

Eye witness. *The same railway station*. We.
Search out the others' errant gunshots

Enchanting for democracy O! Muse you wing it
for shepherds sporting iambic lambs on
the platform so enthralled by Love bo-
peeping his fluttery sonnet in Venus' softest target I

miss my earthly transport, and survive. No
golden glove thrusts from the dust. *Erratum
for Erato*: Nobody drops into the same
device twice. Human error. Petrified watch. Our
sponge of blood drips into *the same device forever*

He breaks off to listen to the
news. Standing at the top
of the stairs he catches
the muffled litanies of *because
we can because*.... Eros-

ion of other people's liberties
he is coerced to give up. He's
given up himself a unilateral

suspension of sovereign operations.
In his refrain of terror 'we' is more than
twice his love story. In most respects
he's an ordinary citizen. He cannot wait

for his promised ID card to stamp out who
he is, twinkles stolen from his lustrous eyes

Self-othering hood Klans one's unbecoming
the obsolete body art of choreographed excess
a video diary that couldn't care more or less

Floating on flesh-hooks in betweenness aloft
who licks the blinding gusset of combat knickers

kicks a pile of fleshly rags shovelled by rubber-
necking rednecks? Instead of thumbprints
they press sweat-stains into the dustiest corners.

A body regime splintered by such loving
inhabits what it shall never possess

A barbed obscenity haunts for an extra ear
the parasitic cyborg whose hearts and minds
surrender to the body's self-absorption.
Under the hood maggots nest like emotion

Through slatted blinds you spy another
writing a stuttery scrawl of spidery infringement.
You chisel each other into pedestal fear,
nailed to combat mottoes, slashed
and slotted in your mirror-script encryption

You're unknown unknowns, improper nouns
once announced in a Cold War Nuke Ode.
Same-selved you live: dead meat on the other's
plate garnished with knowns, lashed to the past

Sirens sing at the fringes of your passage.
Sleep plunders the sickly green of paramedics
under shutters. *History was yesterday*

In the live moment splintering between two deaths
invade this single body and unblade the truth

A Bit Rich

Hardly passing for an event at all, it reflects
the day's rush and the glint of your irises.
Your frog-eyed goggles track our stabs
on the chalk-line, sold to the enemy

The pointed show of your black shoe points
to where the inexplicable explanations lie
curled at the heart of black stone, pulling faces
the hard way between tufts of sky grass
and spoon. Waggle your wings like a tart!

embarrassed by our brittle celibacy, embraced
by your little celebrity! Below, the Earth rolls

from wingtip to wingtip, flecked with targets
rumbling through the Bramleys, as salmon
buck up stream through lemon-juiced runs

Smoking Gun

At the end of the world you are driven away
in the back of the National Limousine, flashing
your legs that wrapped around the international
affair, past flashbulbs of the Final Edition.
You're looking at skinny girls in the magazine

They are sort of you. They kneel in shorts
on a bed as long and thin as your thumb,
tilted muse of cubist accidentals. Raise
your fist to the smoked-out sky, espy the fringe

of the kerb where shadows chase one another,
the low light giving edge to their pursuit.
Mr Bin Laden is not at home. Not emerging

from his cockpit, not rubbing his good eye.
It's not that beard of white smoke again

I no longer turn up for my own recordings.
I simply send along my voice instead

I walk like half a man with rickets,
a flâneur who talks himself into a blind corner
and is pulped by Situationist thugs

I sleep with my eyes open, spy every
ruck and tuck of the bedroom curtain.
I pull my own plug as I feel my rush,
a bonus heartbeat in the vinyl spiral.

I tell my own story, sing myself to death,
an antique pleasure that slips from its sleeve.
I enter this place with repeatable behaviours.
I get smaller and smaller to everyone else.
I'll not learn to wait in my own bated breath

Black night stiffens the resolve of the window.
Wipe-out rain, a bad sound effect of rain, white-
noises your voices out, rustles up a simpler sound
of God's brass neck talking through His hat

Your ruffled reflection raises the ethical question
as you paste words like 'author' and 'authority'
on the board beyond this screen of your becoming

Wind, though outside, sheers your breath away.
On a traffic island in Hardman St., a kneeler torches the night
in Guantánamo orange, grizzled by a protestant cloud.
Police rush on in yellow. Fleshing blue lights on cars
parked as barriers breed darkness in the dark

Smack a lip or two, ruddied up, roughed up for a smile.
Tonight, Condoleezza Rice is being entertained

The foreign secretary, spotting bare-headed top brass,
swipes the tin hat from his head as he follows
down the steps to Iraq's soft tarmac the secretary of state's smile

that's clammed to her face like a category mistake
that dropped down one floor in the lift and emerged
a changeling into the roar of a canvas wind.
Celebrity murderess heads off to a fresh beheading.
Elegant heels lift slender ankles, where he follows

Yawning policewomen guard the spaces in Liverpool
she leaves, a line of orange cones elisions in her diary

Her brain barks orders like a sea captain during desertion.
Abu Ghraib grey ocean lips sharp-toothed cliffs brushed by sun.
The mutineers have taken the dormitory.
As their voices fall asleep, they murmur against her

The lake fashions a gelatinous skin through which
the happy dog plunges into emerald germ-clouds.
Tongues, loose, pulse against the membrane;
a safari suit tangles in a polylingual jungle

She clops by in her new high heels, now
she's discovered the joy of walking taller

You at least work *that* stagger in, the stutter,
the stumble through to a throaty drain
with too much to say – and her bloody kisser.
Jokes in TB's 'farewell' speech are slo-mo mimes
of sea-captains saluting from the bridges of listing

ships in old British films: *our* clipped voices,
their clicking heels. Around the hall, lips curl around
sandwiches – only the cellophane whispers dissent

Caught beneath both wipers,
clinging to the windscreen,
clutches of brittle leaves
that the winds have driven home

Before he's dumped in the bin,
Saddam beats its lid, as fireworks freak;
frigid crimson on the cusp of dusk

Wild roses, mad with warming, blossom
in a springtime of their own sensing

It's Rumsfeld's last 'certain certainty'.
The black cat and its blackest shadow,
thrown by low sun across the carpet, pad by.
I smile to think bits of myself
scattered about the room

His breath takes her beauty away, deep
in his body where language measures the world

One breath it takes to be no longer winning a war.
They cup warm palms over each other's cold knees.
Wind shoulders against the flanks of their house;
windows shiver.
They stand in front of it to stand for themselves

It chimes into rhythm that celebrates itself,
this looking at tomorrow, guiding the eye back
to the time of their looking, a swoon into cracks
between history and memory. She dressed in black

from frisking ponytail to stabbing boot toe. Out-
stretching her impossible heels, he buries himself,
moulding her sighs, in soft mammalian heat

A turn in the tide-patterns turns them up, once only,
after 6000 years, these footprints we misread in the sand:
a woman's deliberate step, her child's capering dance,
until the next tide brushes them away. Reversing
the polarities of a phrase short-circuits the sentence

Under dove-grey skies, dark winter coats resolve into form
two warm smiles. Cheered, re-born into consciousness,
we share the watery patches in the grass, the boggy
dip to the blank lake – then part, chilled. Cars plume

sculpted waves as they push through flooding.
The words in the sentence are like stones laid
deliberate in a row, flush or imbricated

The blushing walls of Haditha overlook the human
covenant: We nestle into one another's beastly warmth

Rainshine shivers on dull platforms
Phone masts silvered in the gloom like shrines gather the chatter
Of the nation in bunches as elderflower tap the breeze

A single oak is fenced in but broken fences
Stitch landscape into the neat motley of Capital
We glide through sward smeared with mustard
Under clouds like smoke from dead fires centuries old
Rainbow umbrellas flip between the cars and the parishless church

Slap-bang in the middle of the country fresh timbers
Naked girders gnaw the ring road of the blue city

The dark girl with long lashes lifts a restless leg to her seat
She reads a biography of our next prime minister
As a tunnel sucks us dry into our own echoes
How English can you get? More so

London

The new twenty-pound note feels crisp as a fake
As Adam Smith lectures us on division
Over a Chelsea bun and a white plastic knife

Through the cafeteria window with its view of the car park
The sun's weak eye at dusk spies the legend
And white men on green signs follow its arrows.
Waiting in the disabled bay between the Nissans

Beneath the limp Swedish flag the lank Union Jack
The Hindu family in pink and salmon grins

We're unstable before this excitation of price tags
A heady Sale as goods levitate before us
We surrender a pony to a dark-eyed migrant labourer
Despite our poor kind speech she gathers none of it
The white disk sinks below the pyramid of returns

Afghanistan

Like a figure in a dream of perfect falling
Like something from somewhere like hell

You were the dark-eyed girl who crept out
Before the pink meat dawn to spy
The growling machines while the whole town
Still dreamt of exactly what she saw

Night vision green flecked with sparks
And clouds of vectoral vapour pouring across
Sun-baked gravel where a human head severe
And severed scarved in crackling plastic
Resurrected. She dived through coils of barbed wire

She ran her oily fingers along the sealed walls
Of the outsiders as though reading their secret script
Or leaving her own

You build from song
an architecture of tumbles

a dance of stumbles on a shelf of air.
You name this the space left by the human.
You excavate Babylon or the strata of resting Jews
and the ribbons of tight ink on Pinkas Synagogue wall
with the surnames' bejewelled rubrication

(Whenever erased they're re-written
the act of their scrubbing
inscribed anew)

Stones leaning splinter through time
for those with no names
possess no death. You ex-
hume the ex-human in human unfinish

for Stephen

The red metronome on Letná hill
sways like a lucky drunkard
on its pedestal above the spires
a restless reminder of rust and wreck.
Or an antique windscreen wiper

describing its arc
upon a plane of smear and rain-wash
heroic in a monochrome movie, tinted red

With each wipe across the screen
the determined visage of the driver clears.
It's Josef Stalin the giant blocks with his pocks
long blown to shatters but he's still there

waving yes and no
to anyone who can see him

for Patricia

The young couples in the crushed Amsterdam bar
dance to Barry White in the old-fashioned way

Later, aloft on Belgian beer, I murmur that I
love you, but then slip away, like the dancers,
into the night, knocking over bicycles chained
to bollards, and singing; into my reverie so far
in which we sit again drinking under the wooden ape

Almost human it grins at us both with more teeth
than the accordion it fumbles. This is all times
becoming a new time which is a now time
becoming all, a swoon through cracks in the paving

where vanished children crouch over hidden play.
Next day, a narrow canal house lips at its reflection;
we stand in front of it to stand for ourselves

Four Poems Against Death

I am small against death and the mourning of history.
　　　　　J.F. Hendry

Later Words on Human Unfinish

Grey screen
framed by window's edge,
a curtain's subtle incursion:

a veiled world
playing out singularities,
complexities. As it

darkens
you're drained by the glow
from the single lamp

Passers-by glance
to tease whatever configures from
the other side

Swift curtains
pull the edges of the world
close in

                Later, in default,
                synthesised voices:

                utter apology in
                human indifference

Later still,
prising

the eye
to the slit between

blank board walls,
regard within

the parched, the cracked
earth; desert:

the hard rhyme of
pairidaeza

Emailing the Dead

i.m. Bill Griffiths

Skeletal announcement
Summons up

       (the crack of bones
       the click of a mouse

Spectral email template
Pre-addressed to the dead one

Ready for our message
From imprescience

Thanatognomic
Ignorance

There's no end to it line-
Break its little one

The dead their own deity it's
Best to offer tactile thanks

Twitching under
Fingerprinting pulse

Little Shovel

for Iain Sinclair

To think through
The tune of the thing

To shiver with joy drive
Pattern against violence

Crueller than cruelty a
Quotation

Awaits new words
To fill it an allograph

Of utter utterance
Caught through the aperture

Of belonging longing
To think a moon

Pressing close to kiss the earth
Over the terraced hill

Dipping toward the turning river
To think outness contests

All the way the outline
Of a shadow that wasn't there

To think accident stumbles evil
Into the poem –

That 'little shovel' scooping his
Liver out to sizzle

– To think with particular and
Articular interruptions

Never to unthink skinned-in
Ecstasies in the poem that

Sees the world as well
As itself

Gravity Be My Friend

before and after Pipilotti Rist

                    , clouds shift

their weight on urban slush underbellies,
the white car bonnet

burns on a squint-edit, no secrets
this afternoon, the earth's map projected

onto heaven, in harsh sun car lamps
re-lit, blue chrome flash blinds me,

crouching grey-white wolf-clouds off,
passion rises in the body like barking

rock'n'roll, sways down the street,
a clarinet practises scales turning to a tune

of a thing from an open window, something
without a head goes head-over-heels,

grey pitted windscreen a shocked wash
of sudden rain, wipers scrape

temporary breach, configure
blotch-moments into solids,

event-sized shapes, both men in front,
loose ties around hot necks, the next clouds'

black rims fringed with greying and blueing,
she slows to light her cigarette, laconic,

steps to a kerb, leather bag over her
shoulder, it slaps her thigh, reminds her,

somewhere inside this body I'm happy, yes, she
walks across the ceiling with her red hair,

negotiating reefs of felt under window clouds,
climbs the ringed bark

into a sky of river,
cools her wrinkled feet

where fish turn to leaves and light, her hair-weed
in the half-tossed tide of the sky,

pulls away
like film that leaves me skinned, I step

from unwounded poise, as crystal light
bursts once more in the street, printing strips

that I peel from the surface of the world
with every newly-minted tread

Another Poem

The scribe of the poem knows nothing
but he embodies every word you hold.
He's not an original. He's a solid
conduit, form rather than wave or
particle. He's left-handed, and his big
fist covers every word once it's formed.
The eyes he turns to us
                        in his mirror
                                  look away.
Careful not to smudge, he crouches low,
reversing the verse, furrowing his plough.
The poem tells of flowers and trees,
naming names you recognise from other
poems, but you can never make them out
in the wild. Did he say 'Wild'? No,
he didn't, as it happens. Neither did
the poem. You're making it up. You think
it should be you alone and the words
agreeing to differ. But you watch his fist
pounding the lines: *Alike the shuddering ball of
flame* or *Print regurgitated pulp*. The poem
has barely recovered from his scratches, yet
you're making to scribble links in its margins,
calming and charmless. Will you then tear
his calligraphy back, peel it off to leave
the wounded poem yours, a dripping pelt?
He fashions the final words. *Waves of feeling rush
towards this hooded moment*. His dream is to be power-
less as the endless poem.

                        Then he
inscribes, in mirror-script: *The scribe of this poem
knows it all*

Yet Another Poem

Incalculable dispersions? The selves I
have a number. Of days now in an art
that is re-made as glaringly brilliant
banging. Art is unmade and laid to
restless drums, banging on about the glare.
Restless brilliance, all wrong, unmindful
in the acts of losing ruthless polarities
in place of space, sufficient ground. It
never lost on either or multiple sides, the
time before, for the setting was seen, a glimpse
of unscheduled action. Now lose the soft
fascination, the definite prosaic self. Losing
surface, the actors pause, surfing the poem and off
on stories, to a place to speak from, circum-
scribed, a stage cluttered with seating.
They have to be arranged to pull a gun
on you, forging a new space, new links.
On those link-sparky tracks, I
don't do that. I make art, unlimited
access, lightning surrogate gun making
language chains the unlikely. A
gun is pulled on the surrogate self, on
screens flat with dialogue, just once,
yards away. The abandoned Coke can
on the wall opposite attracts an art
in which the unsaying saying, once said,
sings. The 'you' that has effects, the
new audience, says again,
                    The props,
or the surrogate props, speak to themselves,
an uncanny overhearing

As Yet Untitled Poem

for John James

I beg you to hear this boy. And hear him out.
His morning poem you're in, now,
is neatly creased as a crisp new shirt, stiff-
backed and clipped on its cardboard torso, posed.

It trips you over the cat from the film you've never
seen, as you search for your spectacles.
I use my enormous brain to seek the signals
they emit. We are both The Prisoner

on this island, Crusoes of overlapping surveillance.
Sleep is where we've come from, captive, a misty place
of drizzled desire and mordant fear. The fog has
lifted, real enough, for the expedition that must

set off for the explanation. Your house-
guest, a sort of vapour that
an opening door dispels, coughs his soft pardons.
Serious poetry is back in town:

the Unfinished *Alba* of the Unknown
Troubadour, whose *vida* is word for word. The
beloved of this lyric is the hero of that epic, where
sometimes I did seek, I beg you now to flee this boy.

Two sections of Words Out of Time: autrebiographies and unwritings

The Given (part one)

I don't remember going to the Grenada in Portland Road, Hove, don't recall the film on show, and don't remember, on the same day, seeing a play, or its plot, or its title. A frame set up, years later, by others. Outside of it there are voices, whispering. Empty landing, tall doors never shut, banging in any wind. The attic, its sloped tar-hair padding, muting all street sounds. On one page, attempts at painting, soaked blots, dried solid. Across the folio, *words*. A carpet of *Daily Heralds* for the blackened man to hump sacks upon through the house to the bunker at the back, in the garden. Coal dust on the doorframe, where the hood catches it. Chorusing thanks over pie-chart fractions. Crawl into the hole under the stairs where browned instructions from the Blitz still hang. Regard a patch called the Egg Field. A gold clock turns under a glass dome. A wasp pullover bobs with a ball by the airbrick. A bedroom, narrowing to this world. Chained from picture rails, oval portraits of tinted babies. Silk slung over banisters. A dozen or so knapped flints pushed into the earth: a Roman road straight across the horses' field, the wheat, the ridge of the Downs. Timbers, pram-wheels, string, scattered around the garden. I don't remember the day I passed cleanliness, the day I drew a pictogram of a body with a blade through it. In the back room, a treadle invites feet that will never reach its gentle whine from the leather dip of the creaking chair. I don't remember riding the trams at Knokke. I don't remember walking the boxer dog Tina. The nude calendar's metal spine will not bend enough for complete concealment. Recaptured on the landing, door swung wide. I don't remember the deaths of Giacometti, Hans Hofmann, Jean Arp. The enemy is always pure machine with flashing lights and monotones. Nazis machine-gun the cheese crates and screaming POWs leap up to their deaths. The pebbly beach beneath the power station will do. An aluminium bowl of wasted food before which feeding is practised with moral intensity. The cool of the wooden hut, a scent of ice-cream that is not ice-cream. Witnessed, it sinks. I don't remember the thunderstorm I watched from my window, lightning flashes over Southwick, flickering, striking ground. After the toad in the witness box, real policemen arrive to investigate stolen buttons, the wrecked foreign car. Tall cream hallway to a room of drums, the shining vibraphone. I don't remember Radio Morse or the term 'key jockey'. Rubber gristle in the mouth for hours, or spat in the toilet, airless gully, escape. I don't remember taking that photograph to use the rest of the film. I don't remember getting Mum's shopping, the day I bought John Lee Hooker's 'Dimples'. I can't remember what I don't remember. I don't remember crossing the Forth Bridge. I don't remember what code I used. The sound of boots on the floorboards, a fragrance of leather and whitewash. The rustling of the bluebell wood, the urine-inducing silence. Dozens of pink stamps, carefully cut from envelopes, franked 'Natal 1899'. A gutted fish on a board: a pantry smell that is the coldness of fish itself. It sits on the window-sill, along with another, whose vitreous leaks from its cracked shell. I don't remember trying to buy *This is Blues* and finding the record sleeve contained only cardboard. I don't remember tracking Radio 260 through the streets of Southwick, the 'common' English of the DJs, the warning that they'd cut up rough if we found them. Outside of it there are voices, evaluating. I don't remember whether I understood that in bringing Apollo 13 back to earth, they would have countered the rising carbon dioxide levels by use of a filter containing lithium hydroxide. The desire to write is the desire to write. I don't remember reading *The Day of the Triffids*. I don't remember watching colour TV. The red blue and white Daz packet, separating red, blue, and white, expanding along the melting body. Magnification without limit. Men ski the wallpaper. I don't remember seeing Portslade on the radar screen, don't remember the visit to HMS Collingwood. Inside the cupboard there are scribbled weather-charts. I don't remember writing a list of stories I'd written. I don't remember being shot at by somebody from a van. I don't remember the good programme about Lenin on the radio. I don't remember debating nuclear warfare in English. I don't remember Kathy getting too close for comfort. I don't remember the day Frank Sinatra retired. I remember the Ruby wine at the Romans, the way the barman would loll his tongue from the side of his mouth as he poured the soupy chemical liquid into Tony's bottles. I don't remember Doll and Arthur's caravan at Selsey. I don't remember witnessing Hitler's last will and testament. I don't remember arguing about Fats Waller. I don't remember trying to define a book. I don't remember writing a history of the avant-garde. I don't remember recording Son House off the radio. I don't remember thinking the prints of Blake ugly when I saw them at the British Museum. I don't remember when I started writing poetry. I don't remember getting a harmonica with Green Shield stamps. Or sea and sand with nothing familiar, perhaps a tent of evangelists.

I don't remember David's bottled fish. I don't remember Emerson Lake and Palmer playing a tribute to Hendrix, a week after his death. I don't remember typing 'Time and Place' in Miss Starkey's flat though I still remember the typeface, the thickness of paper. I don't remember reading *Go Down Moses*. I don't remember calling Sarah 'my beautiful scruff'. Why don't I remember her face streaked with tears? I don't remember eating a photograph of Jennie. I don't remember the Maoist in my novel. I don't remember Ann Starkey's reactions to my novel but I do remember the *words* that describe her reactions to it. I don't remember singing 'Jerusalem' on the way back from the Cardiff Stock Exchange. I don't remember the marketing man who called for a halt to economic growth. I don't remember the TV programme on Stalin. I don't remember seeing a band called Vomit. I don't remember her sighing as I kissed her. I don't remember tea and scones before retiring for sherry, the daughter of the house languidly asking why people *have* to write *such* personal poetry. I don't remember writing to Bob Cobbing. I don't remember feeling illiterate. I don't remember the barrow full of bloodied pigs' heads at Smithfield Market. I don't remember playing my tape of *The Waste Land* to an empty room. I don't remember when poems became a currency. I don't remember a girl called Annie flashing her tits on Toby's houseboat. I don't remember my guts hurting when Linda sat on my lap. Helen didn't remember saying, 'Is it from Dennis?' I don't remember writing a poem about Bill Butler's bookshop. I don't remember Dad's 50th birthday. I don't remember finishing *Ulysses* at 4.40 pm on Wednesday 3 July 1974.

I don't remember the night that was not particularly memorable. I don't remember a band called White Noise. I don't remember buying Barry MacSweeney's poem about Jim Morrison. I don't remember being in a queue at the Occupied Hamburger Bar. I don't remember the Scottish woman who helped me at Metal Box. I don't remember sitting in Southwick Rest Garden to read Wilfred Owen. I don't remember dancing with a girl with a big nose whose brother was a surrealist. I don't remember walking to St Faiths on a crisp sunny Sunday morning.

I don't remember Evelyn. I don't remember that I bought *Bomb Culture* the day I saw Country Joe and The Fish, the doped-up auditorium, the girl in front on downers. I don't remember the girl who was raped in the States telling me, 'I've never seen a poet dancing.' I don't remember Tony arriving at 15 Oakapple Road with a letter from Henri Chopin. I don't remember that Jemma thought herself the greatest poetess since Sappho. I don't remember my provisional *Notes on Literature.* I don't remember the German sailor dead drunk on the steps of the Crown and Anchor. I don't remember turning up at Saturn Studios to find them locked, John Purdy losing his job on the spot, before we went in to record 'The Lover'. I don't remember smoking bum-deal dope and listening to Zappa with John Kemp. I don't remember, when I asked him what he thought of Lee Harwood's writing, Anthony Thwaite replying, 'Rubbish!' I don't remember going to a concert that didn't happen, in a hall that doesn't exist, with a friend who'd gone home last Wednesday. I don't remember playing John Kemp the concrete poetry LP. I don't remember seeing X.J. Kennedy and thinking the sonnet is where professors go to die. I don't remember the clever-dick who wanted to know why the Newhaven-Dieppe crossings were more expensive than the Dover-Calais ones. I don't remember what happened to Dorcas or Tamsin Vaughan-Williams. I don't remember Hilary. I wouldn't remember a man saying of Zappa: 'As an artist he has to produce things that aren't art.' I don't remember seeing *The Bitter Tears of Petra Von Kant* or reading *The Prime of Miss Jean Brodie.* I don't remember arguing with Bob Hodge about the applicability of Kuhn's paradigms to literary history. I don't remember squinting at the smallest penknife in the world. I don't remember David Gascoyne reading 'Hölderlin's Madness'. I don't remember seeing the Doctors of Madness again, not getting it the second time, that blue-haired zeitgeister Kid Strange. I don't remember Jemma fainting on me, with visions of a dead friend. I don't remember reading *Lud Heat* in the swelter of '76. I don't remember Flatfoot at The Alhambra. I don't remember Roger Chapman falling off stage or Trev carrying a broken bottle in case we were attacked again. I don't remember the nice girl from the Joyce and Beckett seminar who sat with me for a few minutes in the bar. I don't remember the disco to celebrate Franco's death. I don't remember the gazebo, don't remember having a blow with Helen in the gazebo, but the Steve Hillage ticket proves that some version of this evening happened. I don't remember that the conversation had been about the death of John Purdy. I don't remember laughing at the statue of the past Mayor of Brighton, with Tony, Tony Lopez and Lee Harwood. I don't remember Dad suggesting journalism and me saying it's a mug's game. I don't remember David Plante lecturing on his masturbatory writing technique. I don't remember complaining that George Barker may have been big in the 1930s, but.... I don't remember ceasing to exist at the party as I became the complete novelist. I don't remember jumbling the verses of 'Travelling Riverside Blues', our first gig. I don't remember that Bob Cobbing still wore knitted ties. I don't remember Jeff Nuttall saying, 'This place is death!' as we cabbed it through Norwich. I don't remember that William Empson had wind.

I don't remember meeting John James and feel vertiginous loss of internal pressure as negative objects throw positive shadows over events I'm not now sure occurred in ways I thought they had only yesterday. I don't remember his laughter was a sneeze of irritation. I don't remember pitching the authority of the text as the subject of itself against the authority of self. I don't recall being willing to accept obscurity. I don't remember doubting that Tim's girlfriend existed. I don't remember Alec the Cowboy at the Penny Farthing Club in Ulverston. I disremember wanting to reach so deep inside that she'd have to let go. I do not remember singing Nick Drake's 'Time Has Told Me'. I don't remember the biggest slagheap in the world. I don't remember what happened to Rita Nightingale, sentenced to 20 years in Thailand. I don't remember declining the role of lead singer in The Painkillers at the benefit for Satan's Slaves in the backroom lock-in after the gig at the Wheatsheaf. I don't remember climbing Chanctonbury Ring, the moon rising ensanguined over the charmed hills, the drink at the George and Dragon with Mick and Val and Tony after.

I don't remember making love, suddenly, dangerously, after going out to vote and getting a soaking. I don't remember seeing Elton Dean at one venue under the vaults of King Street, and Stéphane Grappelli at the Theatre, hours later. I don't remember seeing *Last Year at Marienbad* and recalling the last time I saw it, with Trev and Martine, the year before. I don't remember not meeting Peter Stacey because the clocks had gone back and I don't remember us discussing six basic vowel sounds pitched from a fundamental. I don't remember Mum turning 50, but I called it 'the threshold of old age'. I don't remember offering my spare bed to Paul Stewart, who vowed to emigrate if Thatcher had won by the morning.

from **Arrival**

you arrive as afternoon television
in the fifties curtains pulled grand heroisms
flicker across the pinched grey screen

you're a siren or spy washed ashore from
the U-boat the night-dressed angel
laid out like a traitor under the cliff

the toothpaste white cliff there's no going
back to the big black map of Europe
foghorns drift in the salt-crust mist

not moaning your name it's absent
from these papers I forge to let you in
hoax sister pseudo-sibling Nazi

sabotuese you night-drop onto Southwick Green
tear free your leather caul your parachute
spittled placenta through silk boughs

you limp towards the matinee idol who
mimes my part waiting by the War Memorial
with his flashlight and his notebook guilty

with elegy edgy with guilt the secret
code-word to end all death is balanced
on the tip of his errant tongue

*

Standing by

for my father

> There was a time for tears,
> When Death stood by us, and we dared not weep.
> David Raikes

'Chuting through darkness the drop mourns itself
Morphine thickens the glassy eye farther into
Its own refractive density in this world which

Is not the case the dream-chatter of the dead
Meaningless encased in his own deafening dome
Poetry does nothing here the earpiece vibrates

Breathe shallow like aircrew watching gulls
Wheeling above long lines laid out as overhead wires
Inhaling hollow crackling rattling nothing left to say

Nobody to address mouthpiece dry and formal
The soft 'Oh!' coughs from the last breath a message
Elegy lost in action on the outskirts of an event

Fictional Poems from
A Translated Man: René Van Valckenborch and his double oeuvre

from masks *(supposedly from the Walloon)*

3

modern mask ghana

front view

    mounted on a wall

spout moon mouth of
spirit language gushes
you! look! listen!

(sketches of
face-shapes are hardwired into
our recognition drives)

eyes convex ovals hold
a-human twin slits a hint
of surveillance

from the other side (you've
been there you know there's nothing
no one there but your slightest movement

doubts you) metal cheeks of peppered
hammer blows eyebrows of
bevel pits bolted to skin

in symmetry above/below eyes
all bound by a circular band
earth-red in which wave-forms play

pure energy scored seashore frown
on a sanded forehead (bristles
of sea-beard rhyme beneath)

three tears filed free of
varnish wash pearl
pips from the fruited eyes

but above the top & tailed fish
scaled nose a forehead
of wooden hair strains

a frontal lobe
nudging into the world
an invasive fist of mind

that echoes the mouth
which rather than speaks
sucks

into its black hole
a whirlpool withdrawing
its eternal guttering moan

9

navajo

fingers
        ruffle the
scalp its matted horsehair
soul birth

wrap a hide too
small for saddle into
bare life face

gouge eyeholes
mouth hole but nose
– nostrils – not drilled

paint white zig
zags down one cheek
that breathes under them

as they mould a man
plant a single feather
for affect ready

for the plains alert
to sky's tremulous
messages where

birds peck this wig
for nests beaks poke
eye peeped worm holes

stab eye as mask becomes
body itself in(-)
animate art life god

with no voice or vice
cast-off man staggers
against horizon a sky

trickling sand a landscape
gifting abyss until such
aloneness engenders

heroics enacts wind
revives riverbed
summons cloud mr

rainwater his
dry quill rustling with
distant unfelt breeze

      he falls to earth
      & human sweat
      flushes laughing

15

gas mask first world war flanders

strapping your head into
the theriomorphosis of the grub
a rubbery frown folds over yours

gaze of supernal sunken
eyes glazed rings of the
pneuma's vigil over mud

in place of mouth a divine cylinder
a proboscis extrudes
a can of maggots

deep rattling of the sieved voice
through perforations a frigid
filtering of tellurian poisons

from **The Light** *(supposedly from the Flemish)*

The Word

> *We are an echo of an echo of the sky.*
> Jaan Kaplinski

Sky.
Sky the hue of a sick egg unbroken.
A half-formed beak. Talons clawing at fog. Mottled rug
flung over the furniture of day. A chair leg's betrayal.
Everything out of place. The sky could go on
displaying itself forever like this. Flaking
immeasurably. I could go on describing it forever.
Verbing its adjectival noun adverbally. Stop. The poem
could go on forever. It tells us the best way
of going on. Go. On forever turn the sky into something else
a semblance of itself the poem's. A fish winching
itself across a screen of smudged clarities.
It's taking place in the spaces of the poem.
Smoke for blocked chimneys. Shallows of blue
in the depths open up. Like the poem. Atlas
dictionary thesaurus tugging at my sleeve.
A spasm across a keyboard. I've not used the word yet.
The word underlined in every draft you reject.
The word that rides the tongue. A tongue riding
the word is the word. Moistening the sky it forms.
Anything that enters the sky is the sky.
Anything that enters the poem is the poem.

from EUOIA: European Union of Imaginary Authors

Austria Sophie Poppmeier (1981-)

Book 1 Poem 1

All propositions in poems
are fictions I know
except in this one, otherwise
why would I write it now?

It sits where I sit enlanguaging
what it enlanguages at the centre
of 'my fabulous continent'
which, like the middle of an

old record overplayed clumsily,
is a loose black hole that's
unfit for purpose, whose purpose was
to repeat what's already been performed.

I lie in wait for the new lyric
which lies low, lying like hell
in heavenly form. It echoes
my chants to change my life.

www.ingramcontent.com/pod-product-compliance
Lightning Source LLC
Chambersburg PA
CBHW031150160426
43193CB00008B/317